FRESHWATER FISHING

FRESHWATER FISHING

Ray Ovington

ILLUSTRATIONS BY THE AUTHOR

HAWTHORN BOOKS, INC.
Publishers/New York
A Howard & Wyndham Company

AN INDIAN PRAYER

HEAR us, O Great Spirit in the sky. Our people are very old people. We lived in this land thousands of moons before the White Man came. His way of life differed from ours. For many seasons there was bitter strife between us. Now, there is peace but the heart of the Red Man is sad, for the White Man has destroyed many of Nature's most bountiful gifts and has forgotten that all things come from Mother Earth and go back to her.

O Great Spirit, bring to our white brothers the wisdom of nature and knowledge that if her laws are obeyed this land will again flourish and grasses and trees grow as before. Guide those who through their councils seek to spread the wisdom of their leaders to all people. Heal the raw wounds in the earth and restore our clear and beautiful streams. Bring again the sparkling waters from our springs and restore to our soil the richness which strengthens men's bodies and makes them wise in their councils.

Wyoming Wildlife

CONTENTS

ACKNOWLEDGMENTS *xi*

PREFACE—SPORT FISHING AND THE FISH *xiii*

INTRODUCTION *3*

1 SPIN FISHING *7*

    Operating the Tackle   7
    Perfecting Spin Casting   9
    Striking, Playing and Landing the Fish   17
    Putting Your Tackle Away   18
    Recommended Spinning Tackle for Average
      Freshwater Fishing   19

2 BAIT CASTING *20*

    Bait-Casting Rod   20
    Bait-Casting Procedure   23

3 FLY-FISHING   26

Learning to Set Up Gear   26
Learning to Make the Casts   31
Variations on the Fore-and-Aft Cast   36
Striking, Playing and Landing   42

4 TERMINAL TACKLE   45

Lure Selection and Artificial Flies   45
Natural Baits   52
Basic Terminal Rigs   55

5 TACKLE CARE AND REPAIR   62

6 ACCESSORIES   65

Water Transportation   65
Footgear   66
Jackets   67
Tackle Box and Lure Containers   67
Staff and Nets   68
Fish Keepers and Bait Boxes   68

7 A PANFISHING EXCURSION   70

8 GOING AFTER LARGER FISH   79

Pickerel   79
Bass   86
Walleyed Pike   97
Pike and Muskie   100
Trout   102
Cutthroat and Steelhead   109
Salmon   111
Shad   114

9 MOST POPULAR GAME FISH SPECIES   *115*

    Trouts   116
    Salmon   124
    Bass   127
    Pike   128
    Shad   132
    Catfish and Panfish   133

APPENDIXES   *137*

    Planning Your Fishing Trip   137
    Sources of Fishing Information   138
    Maps That Aid the Angler   140
    Cleaning Your Fish   141

GLOSSARY   *143*

BIBLIOGRAPHY   *145*

INDEX   *147*

ACKNOWLEDGMENTS

This is my twenty-fifth book on outdoor recreation. Twelve of these have been about fishing, the latest being *Tactics on Trout* (New York: Alfred A. Knopf, 1969) and *Tactics on Bass* (New York: Alfred A. Knopf, forthcoming). Two recent books of similar interest were published by the Stackpole Company, *Introduction to Bait Fishing* (1973) and *Basic Fly Fishing and Fly Tying* (1974). *How to Take Trout*, published originally by Little, Brown in 1952, has been recently reprinted and updated by Freshet Press, New York. Since basic fishing information on fishing rigs and techniques is universal, I am indebted to these publishers for the use of information that has been incorporated in this book. Thanks for material concepts and specific information written for this book go also to magazine publishers who have published articles under my name, such as *Field and Stream, Outdoor Life, Sports Afield, True, Argosy, Elks, The Fly Fisherman, Trout Magazine, Pennsylvania Angler,* and many other publications.

I will always be indebted to the *New York World Telegram and Sun* for publishing my daily column "Outdoors." This assignment offered trips all over the globe and experiences that few could ever hope to be granted.

Thanks, too, to the guides, outfitters, conservation officials, travel agents, tackle retailers, and fellow anglers who have contributed to my experience as a sportsman and angler. My Dad gets an extra thanks.

PREFACE
SPORT FISHING AND THE FISH

What is the motivation behind the fact that every year forty million freshwater anglers buy licenses and go fishing? It is certainly not to provide food for the table, since fish markets and frozen-food counters have all kinds of fish, cleaned, frozen and neatly wrapped as well as packages of precooked fish.

At first it would appear that fishermen want to have fun and match their wits with the fish. Deeper than this urge is the desire to return to nature. To the pond. To a stream. Away from cities and crowds. Back to the basic contact with the natural environment from which man emerged. When we fish, we are our own boss, answerable only to Mother Nature, a fascinating gal to know.

According to historians, sport fishing has been with us for at least two thousand years. Most fishing in early times was to obtain food for the family. Today the sport and art of fishing enjoys at least two hundred years of refinement, both in aesthetic appreciation and in the improvement of tackle and technique. You can still go forth with a pole cut from a sapling tree, a string, a store-penny hook and a can of worms and you'll catch fish. But the real joy is in using beautifully designed rods, reels, lines, terminal tackle and a myriad of artificial lures. With these you will not only catch more fish but also have more fun. There is nothing like going astream or on the pond with the right gear, knowing how it works, and armed with the tricks, tips and hints to make your fishing trip more productive.

Where to go? Almost anyplace where there is water! Some of the sportiest fish may not reside in the lake or stream nearest your house. But unless you live in the desert, a short ride or bike pedal will take you to some form of natural water. And there will be some fish there. If you live in the Northeast, for example, a nearby pond may contain catfish, panfish, even bass. There will be trout in the cool streams and deep lakes, perhaps even landlocked salmon. Atlantic salmon fill the rivers of Maine and the eastern Canadian provinces along with smallmouth bass, pike and muskies. If you live in the Southern states you'll find good largemouth bass, catfish and panfish in almost every river. In the Midwest, you go for bass and trout, and pike and muskies. On the West Coast, you'll encounter sea-run cutthroat, steelhead and rainbow trout, as well as many species of salmon. There are good bass lakes in the states of Oregon and Washington. Later I will go into an in-depth study of the various species, their habitats, attractions and the modes of angling for them.

In fishing you have the opportunity to engage in an activity where there are few constants as in sports such as tennis, golf or in any of the team games. In these sports the boundaries are prescribed. The only restrictions in fishing are the game laws. Water, weather, and seasonal conditions are never the same, nor are the types and kind of water, the varieties of fish habits, moods, feeding and striking abilities.

You'll find that each kind of fishing offers its own particular thrills. When you are able to cast a dainty dry fly over the glassy trout pool of a mountain stream and entice a trout into leaping at it, there is a sensation that will be long remembered. The bass that bursts out of a crop of lily pads to pounce on your plug will make you jump in response. The little sunfish that grabs a worm dangled over the end of the dock can be a lot of fun as well. Many of the world's most sophisticated anglers still find a special thrill in panfishing even though they have been used to fighting giant tuna or big-deep monsters. Certainly, the first time you view an Atlantic salmon jumping over a twelve-foot waterfall, you'll wonder what that fish can do to your frail fly-fishing tackle.

There are many fishing adventures ahead for you, whether they be a simple jaunt to a neighborhood lake or a well-planned trek to distant waters. Fishing, you'll find, is full of wonderful surprises.

In this book, I present a good deal of information that can be the springboard to further knowledge-by-fishing. No one book can ever tell it all. The best book available is *The Compleat Angler*, the classic by Izaak Walton, published in the eighteenth century. You can take off from there. The New York Public Library lists over ten thousand books about fishing. This basic book guides you with the use of pictures and diagrams. Follow them and you will begin to know your tackle and techniques before you actually go fishing.

The oldest form of human communication found on ancient temples and in caves are stick figures of human beings engaged in different activities. Today's children begin to draw using the stick figure. I have used this technique to show the motions of the hand, wrist, arms and body in conjunction with tackle, in step-by-step instruction in the actual casting routines. Following the principle "the simpler the better," I believe that the stick figure is most appropriate for this type of instruction. You will see the steps to be taken and mastered. Each diagram has a caption describing the motion.

FRESHWATER FISHING

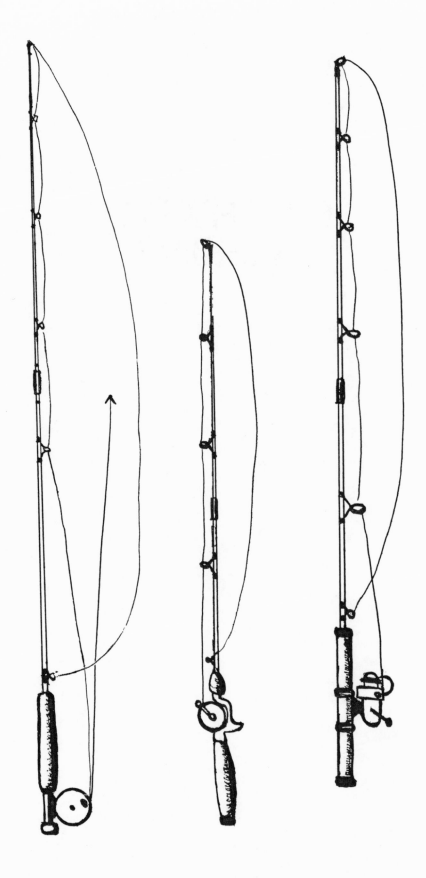

INTRODUCTION

BUYING TACKLE

The purchase of tackle, like the buying of anything else that is important, should be made only after serious planning. Naturally the tackle you buy at the beginning of your fishing career will not be the only tackle you ever buy. Over a period of time you'll discover brands and types of equipment that you prefer. You'll also wear out or lose equipment and have to replace it.

Good fishing tackle is not cheap. You can buy cheap tackle, but you'll find that buying good equipment is, in the long run, the most inexpensive way to equip yourself properly. I always tell beginners, or parents who are buying the first equipment for their children, not to buy cheap tackle. It is usually inefficient or breaks down easily and quickly. There is nothing as discouraging to the beginner as malfunctioning equipment.

It is better to buy one good rod and one good reel than three cheap ones that will not function well. After a few years or even one full season of fishing, you'll develop tastes for specific kinds of gear. Then you can buy what is best for you. Care for it well, and it will last through many years of even the hardest usage. You'll get to know it and it will always function and be dependable. This will offer you the freedom to concentrate on your fish finding and presentation techniques rather than being concerned with the operation of your gear.

In dealing with the actual tackle recommendations, I will outline a basic set of specifications, general as they are (and must be), to be your guide in the combinations of gear that are recommended for various specific fishing demands. Take the list to the tackle store and look over the gear on the shelves and counters. Talk over your fishing prospects with the tackle clerk and get his recommendations. Buy your tackle in a regular fishing-tackle store where there are specialists to help you. There is a big difference in the service you'll get in such stores in contrast to that offered by the big general store or discount outlet which sells everything.

The specialized tackle store is often a mecca for other anglers and members of the local rod and gun club. You will get to know many fishermen who will be happy to help you, including sharing where-to-go information for the best fishing. You may not get the general-store discounts but you'll profit in many other ways.

The real adventure of tackle buying is in the lure department. Here you'll see the inventive genius of the designers of a seemingly endless number of lures. Lures fall into definite classifications. At first you'll be tempted to buy many more lures than you actually need. Here again, refinement and discrimination will develop as you progress.

SETTING UP THE GEAR

The proper routine for setting up your gear will seem quite involved at first. But after the first few times, the routine will become almost automatic. There is a logical procedure to follow, just as there is when you disassemble your gear to put it away. If you bear this in mind, you'll have a minimum of time spent in tackle tinkering, leaving the maximum time for your fishing.

This part of the sport also involves tackle maintenance and proper storing, oiling and minor care. After the season is over, there is the job of complete cleaning, repairing and replacement. It is better to keep your tackle in good order so that setup time is kept to a minimum. It would be quite foolish to merely throw the gear in the car and then, on the fishing site, discover that you have left an important item behind in your closet or that the reel you hoped to fish with needed prior inspection and possible repair.

Keep your rods in their cases until the actual time of fishing. Your reel is kept in a case or a box and your lures and terminal gear in a tackle box. (See Chapter 6 on accessories.) The best tackle box is a fairly large one which will also carry the reels. I own a large tackle box in which I keep everything. When I go to the fishing location, this box, complete with repair tools, oils and whatnots, is "home base" in the car. If I'm going to fish by wading, I take only what I'll need for that trip from the stock box. Same goes for the boating trip. Actual setting up is not started until I'm ready to fish.

I have described in detail the step-by-step procedure of setting up the three types of fishing outfits (spinning, bait casting and fly-fishing) in Chapters 1, 2 and 3, which deal with casting instruction.

LEARNING TO CAST

Learning to cast with your fishing gear is akin to learning to swing a golf club. It requires a synchronized set of steps made by your hand, wrist, arm and body that are directly related with the action of gear in your hand. As in the golf swing, the element of timing is perhaps the most important part. The beginning of the swing of the rod, which creates the pressure bend of the rod, the forward swing and the release of line are the main actions to learn. The proper way to do it is to first become acquainted with the operation of the reel and the handling of the line once the rig is all set to operate for you. Then the casting rhythm is tried. A short cast is made merely to set the routine. Gradually more power is exerted to bring into full performance both the tackle and the caster.

Armed with a balanced set of gear, as is described, let's take each type of gear separately. We begin with spinning, followed by bait casting and finally fly-fishing, which is the most difficult and requires a subtle handling of rod, reel and line and your body.

SPIN FISHING 1

OPERATING THE TACKLE

First of all, when you open the box with the new reel in it, fill out the guarantee and read the directions of its operation carefully. Then read it all again. It is described in words and diagrams far better than I could describe it here. Besides, there are any number of reels you might buy, so for me to detail the operation of setting each one of them up for casting would be rather unnecessary. For general reference, see Fig. 1–1 for illustration of the various parts of typical reels.

Suppose you have bought a standard-label reel such as the Garcia in the open-face type. This reel comes with an extra spool. The spools are instantly detachable and make it possible to really have two or more reels in one, since at any given time you can switch from reel to reel and thus use varied weight lines. In the better stores, the clerk usually spools on the line for you, but if you have to do it yourself, make sure that you roll the line on directly without a twist in each revolution as is shown in Fig. 1–2. For trout and bass fishing load one spool with a four-pound test, the other with an eight-pound test line. This is sufficient to handle all weight lures.

As you will read in the reel directions manual, you thread the line through the closed bail on the reel, through the groove made to carry the line. Now attach the reel in line with the guide on the first handle section of the rod. Take the tip section of the rod, rub the ferrule on your nose to oil it a bit and insert the section into the butt-section ferrule by first lining up the guides so that you will not twist the sections once it is inserted. Twisting the

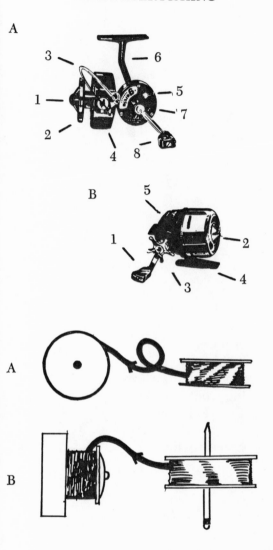

A

B

A

B

FIGURE 1-1. TYPICAL OPEN AND CLOSED-FACE REELS FOR SPINNING

A is a conventional open-face spinning reel, which is the type the author recommends.

Here are the functioning parts as labeled: 1] Drag adjust nut (spools are instantly removable for quick line change). 2] Spool. 3] Bail pickup. 4] Roller. 5] Antireverse lever. 6] Frame foot mounting. 7] Gear housing. 8] Crank.

B is the conventional closed-face reel to be used on spinning rods, bait-casting rods or even fly rods.

Here are the functioning parts as labeled: 1] Crank. 2] Line outlet shield (cover). 3] Star drag adjustment. 4] Foot. 5] Line release lever (for casting).

FIGURE 1-2. SPOOL LOADING

A Wrong. If you load the spool this way, you will make loops that cause tangles when you cast.

B Right. Spool the line on directly without loops. Wind the line on by reeling in with the reel mounted on the butt section of the rod for ease of operation. Have your partner hold the line spool and let it revolve on a pencil. With the line wound on this way, with even tension, you are ready to fish!

sections forms grooves that will cause much trouble later. Also, when taking the rod apart, be careful not to twist it for the same reason. Do not bend the rod when pulling the sections apart. This strains the joints and tends to bend or loosen the ferrules. These are all simple precautions but necessary ones to make that rod last and do its job well for you.

With the rod assembled, the reel in the center of the handle, and the line fed from the reel, pull out line against the reel click drag and thread the line through the rod guides. Once through the tip-top, attach a snap swivel to the line using the clinch knot. (See the discussion of knots in Chapter 4 under "Basic Terminal Rigs.")

Now you are ready for business.

For practice, put on a lightweight object just to simulate a weighted lure. A stick will do, or anything handy that is not more than an ounce in weight. Draw out about a foot of line, stand up and hold the rod out in front of you. As your reel instruction book indicated, pick up the line in your index finger and open the bail. Point the rod up slightly. The weight is dangling from the rod tip.

Now merely let go of the line. The weight will drop. Look at the reel. There is no backlash. Only the needed amount of line came from the spool. That is the basic principle of the spinning reel. Casting it is as easy as what you have just performed. Repeat the process up to the time of line release and then release it again to get the feel.

To cast, first do a practice dry run. With the line in your finger and the bail open, lift that rod from the horizontal to the vertical with a bit of a swing upward and then bring it down again. Feel the line pull at your finger? Do this a few times, just to get the swing of it. On one of the downward swings, let go of the line at just about the horizontal point. See it cast out in front of you? To reel it back in, you merely crank the reel handle and the bail closes over the line and in she comes! Simple?

To make the cast well, study the diagrams and captions which appear later in the chapter. Note the diagrams of both the right and wrong release time and the results. Don't let that bad habit get started. Keep your casts flat and straight to the target.

PERFECTING SPIN CASTING

Spinning is the most modern mode of tackle and casting. The tackle was developed in Europe and came to America prior to World War II. Spinning reels were developed on a very simple principle in order to create an easier way of casting than was available for lure fishing with the conventional bait-casting reel. By merely turning the reel spool 180 degrees and allowing the line to loop off the end of the spool, rather than having to unwind it off the rolling spool, a completely new system was developed (see Fig. 1–3). Here, in one simple step, the age-old trouble of backlashes was eliminated. With the line falling off as casting pressure dictated, a frictionless flow of line was possible, thereby allowing lighter lures to be cast accurately and far. For many years, it looked as if spinning was going to put bait casting

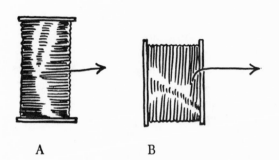

FIGURE 1–3. SPOOL TYPES

A shows the conventional barrel position for unwinding the line.

B shows the open-end position of the same barrel that allows the line to coil off the end of the rim.

A   B

on the shelves of the museum. But bait casting has not only survived, it has become even more popular. The two methods each have their own place in angling. Spinning has grown to be of great prominence in both fresh- and saltwater angling. You will see the reasons why as you go through the steps of performing the spin cast and later catching and playing fish with this gear.

The open-face reel was the original creation. This was followed by the closed-face reel which has also become quite popular. See Fig. 1-1. This angler, however, still holds to the open-face reel for many reasons which will become obvious through the instruction. In my opinion the placing of the one face over the front of the spool restricts the line flow. I do not use

FIGURE 1–4.

Baitcasting reels and baitcasting rods are best for trolling, since the rods are shorter and stiffer, thus offering better hooking strength. The reels are, size for size, generally stronger and have better drags than spinning reels. Larger reels can be used for trolling for big fish such as pike, muskellunge, and Pacific salmon. When casting with heavy live bait, e.g., wrapped chubs or suckers in muskellunge or pike fishing, the bait casting outfit is preferred over the spinning gear.

the closed-face reel and I don't even own one. The description of its operation is included only for the sake of those who might like to try it (see Figs. 1-5 through 1-7).

FIGURE 1-5. HAND POSITION: CLOSED-FACE REEL

This is the manner of gripping the closed-face reel when it is mounted on a bait-casting reel with an offset handle. Note that the thumb falls easily on the release lever that controls the release of the line during the forward swing of the cast.

FIGURE 1-6. PUSH-BUTTON REEL

The push-button reel is basically a spinning reel with a cone-covered stationary spool as in the open-face model. Instead of a bail pickup, which requires the user to pick up the line in the index finger each time he casts, the push-button reel has a lever with which to release the line at the proper time. The reel comes equipped with star drag, antireverse handle and is easy to learn to use. It can be used with the conventional light bait-casting rod and the proper weights of spinning rods. This is an exceptional rig for bait fishing as well as trolling and lure casting.

FIGURE 1-7. ADJUSTING DRAG ON CLOSED-FACE REELS

To reduce drag tension, back up handle about ¼ turn. To regain original drag tension, turn handle forward.

WHAT IS SYNCHRO-DRAG?

The Star Drag is synchronized with another instantly adjustable drag built into the handle mechanism. No need to touch the drag wheel when a big fish makes a desperate lunge—just turn the handle back to reduce drag instantly.

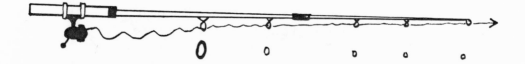

FIGURE 1-8. LINE GUIDES ON SPINNING ROD

FIGURE 1-9. ROD FLEXING

This is an illustration of the flexing motion of the rod. The rod is held at the horizontal position and only pressure (up and down) is exerted. Flex the tip of the rod and make the weight begin to travel as it will when you perform the cast. Flex several times to get the feel of the action. Starting slowly and easily, increase the pressure and note the change necessary in the timing due to the additional pull from the weight on the rod tip. As you will see later, this same pressure is felt when the rod is at the vertical position.

The spinning rod is quite different from the bait-casting or fly rod. Since the reel hangs down (the open-face reel) under the handle, the guides are mounted on the bottom of the rod. You'll notice that the line guides are very large near the reel, gradually becoming smaller as they approach the tip of the rod (see Fig. 1-8). This is necessary, since the line, as it feeds from the end of the reel spool, is coming off in coils, and too rapid a restriction of the line would seriously affect the speed of the line through the guides. Also of importance in casting is the flexing action of the rod. Fig. 1-9 shows this motion.

Rod Grip

As you can see from Fig. 1-10, showing the typical spinning rod handle with the reel mounted hanging down, the rod must be gripped with the stem of the reel straddled between the second and third fingers. You must grasp the rod handle gently.

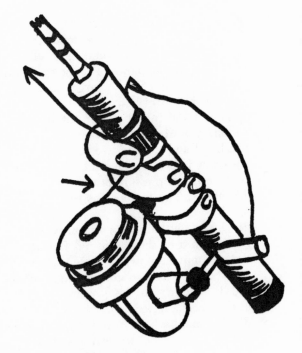

FIGURE 1-10. GRIPPING THE SPINNING ROD

The right hand is gripping the spinning rod with the stem of the reel between the second and third fingers. The grip should be relaxed so that the wrist is free to move and act. The forefinger grasps the line lightly as well as the rod handle for casting pressure. At the moment of release of the line, the index finger lets go of the line and the line slips or is pulled off the finger section for the cast.

Try not to develop the habit of a tense grip on any tackle, since this will soon tire you. There is no need for hand tension at all. Gripping the handle and coming around the reel in this fashion releases the forefinger which will now be free to touch the spool and thus control the line flow. This is the counterpart of the action of the thumb in line control in bait casting, but it is much simpler. Grasp the rod so that your thumb is resting comfortably on top. Do not twist the hand so that you can see your finger-nails.

With the proper rod grip, you are ready to cast. The spin casting sequence for short distances is illustrated in Fig. 1-11. For longer distances, use the power cast detailed in Fig. 1-12. Control of distance is discussed further in Fig. 1-13 on control of line release.

Retrieving the Line

The next thing to learn, before going into the business of actual fishing, is the retrieving of the line from the cast. To begin, close the bail over the line by starting to crank the handle. The mechanics are automatic. You start to retrieve with the rod in a position just a few inches above the horizontal so that a little tension is on the line and the rod will cushion a sudden pull. If

FIGURE 1-11. CASTING SEQUENCE

Note that all through the sequence the forearm is kept horizontal and all the action is in the hand. The power cast, which exhibits hand, wrist and arm movement, is described in Fig. 1-12.

1] This is the initial power lift from the stationary horizontal position of the rod. The hand and the rod are both "flat." As the arrow indicates, the rod begins to bend as the upward pressure of the hand brings this about. The lure begins to move outward.

2] This is the halfway position where the blacked-in area shows the rod flexing and the lure moving upward. Note that during this stage the hand is not moving, and the rod is reacting to the pressure that has already been exerted on it.

3] The final back pressure is applied as the hand reaches the vertical position in a pressure push. The arrow shows the direction of the rod flex and the path of the weight as it swings well down.

4] With the lure down and the rod bent to the extreme back position, the hand is snapped gently forward, which causes a reverse of the movement of the preceding diagram. The lure travels up and over the tip of the rod and, when it reaches its final point as shown, it is time to release the line by allowing it to slip off the index finger. (In the case of the closed-face reel, you merely push the button to release the line at this point.)

5] Here you see the relaxed descent of the rod and the release of the line as it goes straight out from the rod tip and begins to drop down to the water. The final position of the cast is exactly the same as the beginning—the horizontal position with the hand and rod "flat."

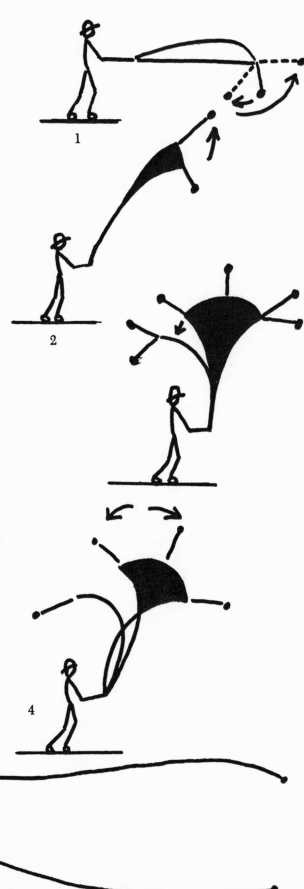

FIGURE 1-12. POWER CAST

This is a diagram of the hand action of the spin cast. The cast you have just performed in Fig. 1-11 is good enough for short distances, but when you want to begin to reach out a bit farther, or exert more pressure if you are using a light lure, you bring the forearm into play as in sequence A.

A] Note the horizontal starting position. The first power is exerted by the hand and a slight movement of the forearm. The final push backward finds the hand near the vertical position and the forearm almost vertical. Next comes the forward snap, at which time the line is released, and then the return to the horizontal position of rest.

B] This is the same routine again, but notice that the whole arm is involved now for a very powerful cast.

As you become familiar with your tackle and its action in relation to your hand, forearm and full arm, you'll likely use a combination of all three of these movements and parts of your arm for an easy cast which will not tire the wrist. The most important element is the exertion of pressure up and back and then forward—through line release—and then down again. Practice this many times, but again, take it easy. Don't try to hit a homer on the first trials.

you like, you can raise this almost to the vertical. It is your choice. When actually fishing you have better control if you retrieve with the rod at about a two-o'clock angle. As the lure comes in close, you can gradually lower the rod tip so that the lure remains in the water until the very last moment.

The horizontal position is also a good one when you are manipulating the rod to give action to the lure. Do this by pulling back suddenly and then lowering the rod to make the lure move up and down in the water.

The retrieve is diagramed in Fig. 1-14. Retrieving tricks for fishing are covered in later sections on fishing techniques and lure handling.

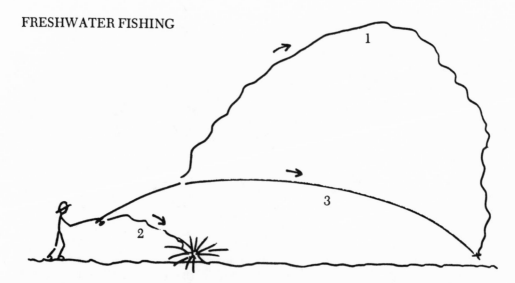

FIGURE 1-13. LINE RELEASE

The most difficult part of the spin cast is the timing of the line release. If you let go of the line too soon, the lure will take off into the air as shown in [1]. This may get the lure to the desired point, but if there is a wind, it will disrupt your direction. Distance is practically impossible to control. The third problem is that there will be much too much slack line on the water which you will have to reel in quickly before a fish strikes, or if you are using a sinking lure in shallow water, it will snag on the bottom before you can start retrieving. As a matter of fact, when fishing in shallow water the cast must be flat, and you begin the retrieve a split second before the lure hits the water on the normal cast [3].

[2] indicates that the release of the line is much too late. As shown in previous diagrams, the angle of the lure in relation to the rod is important to note and feel. If you wait too long for the release, the lure will splash down in front of you, well short of its target.

[3] shows the proper direction of the lure from the rod tip. This is the nice flat cast that is directional, saving on slack line and accurate, plus the fact that it is easy to control as to distance and also immediate retrieve.

To control distance, try snubbing the line before the lure begins to fall at the point shown in the diagram. To do this you merely place your index finger on the very lip of the spool. This retards and/or stops the line from coming off the spool. Note that if you really snub the line tight, the lure pulls at you and bounces down into the water. Try this a few times to get the "feel" and you will always be able to control a lure that is headed for the brush and snags. It is surprising, but believe it or not, you'll soon be controlling those casts to within inches of your selected target.

Take it easy now. Don't try to make full-distance casts yet. Get to know your outfit, so that its operation is almost second nature to you. One day, or rather, one night soon, you may be fishing in total darkness. You'll have to perform all this without looking.

What you have just begun to master is the vertical cast. The sidewinder cast is essentially the same, only the rod is pointed at the target, and instead of bringing it straight up to your eye in the vertical, you swing it in the horizontal line, being careful that no one is near you and that you are clear of brush or snags. This cast is only recommended when you want to throw the lure under an overhang or there is a tree limb over your head. Stick to the vertical cast for most of your fishing. It is much more accurate as you will find out.

Now it's up to you. To write any more or draw more pictures would complicate it unnecessarily. Start practicing. Fifteen good solid minutes should make you an expert. That's why spinning is so popular. It is the easiest method! And when you realize the variety of lures you can pitch great distances, you'll be glad you learned to spin!

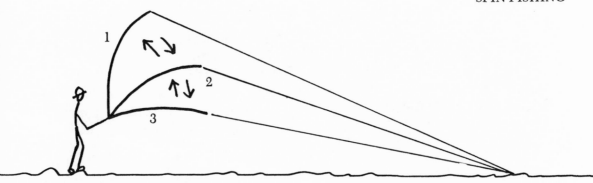

FIGURE 1-14. THE RETRIEVE

Position [3] is that of the normal retrieve. However, position [2] is also recommended, since the bent rod gives a little tension against the line for even spooling as well as a cushion against the strike of the fish. Position [1] can be used most of the time for safety, and especially when using sinking lures in shallow water or when it is desired to keep the lure right on the surface. Positions [2] and [3] also keep the line from snagging brush, grass or pads as you are retrieving. To give the lure action on the retrieve, you can snap the rod from the near vertical (two o'clock position) down to position [3] or to the horizontal for the most extreme effects.

STRIKING, PLAYING AND LANDING THE FISH

Here we bring into play the built-in features of the spinning reel that make playing the fish more fun, easier and very efficient.

First, preset the drag of the reel spool to just under the breaking strength of the line. One way to realize the terrific amount of reserve power in the rod you are using is to attach the line to a solid object and back away about fifty feet. Then raise the rod tip against the strain of the tied line and bend the rod full against it until the drag lets go and the line goes out from the reel. See? You have a large amount of reserve power, even with a very light rod and line. Now you can feel the amount of safety in striking your fish. The light spinning rod, with its exceptionally well-designed margin of spring, and the lightest line are sufficient for playing much bigger fish than you might have thought. Performing this simple experiment will tell you a lot about your tackle and its possibilities. This will give you the knowledge of just how hard you can fight a fish under given conditions or how easily you can haul it through brush and snags or even the fastest of water.

There is another part to this experiment. Point the rod straight at the line as it is attached. Now pull directly without using the cushion of the rod. The line breaks easily. This shows that you must keep that rod tip up or in the horizontal position, back at right angles to the battle. In Chapter 3 on fly-fishing I show the three positions of the fight and explain why the near vertical is the safest and best.

At times during the battle with the fish, you may want to tighten the drag on the reel spool so that control of the line in relation to the rod pressure is easier. If you do this, remember to again set the drag to a much lighter striking position for your next encounter.

When landing the fish, keep the rod up or back and ease the fish down into the net. Do not make scooping passes at it. Usually there is enough of a final kick in the fish under fright to make a fast dash to freedom. To avoid this, don't scare him with the net, but rather let him slide into it after you have the net submerged. In Chapter 6 on accessories I discuss the various types of nets and their use.

PUTTING YOUR TACKLE AWAY

Breaking down your tackle should not be taken literally. For orderliness and to make sure everything is OK for the next outing, break down the rig by detaching the lure from the snap swivel and put it back in the tackle box. If you are merely stacking the rig for another trip in a few hours and do not need to break down the rod and put it away, you can attach the swivel to the keeper ring just ahead of the rod handle (on most good rods). This is better than attaching the swivel and snap to the tip-top guide at the end of the rod. Metal-to-metal scratches should be avoided, and that guide above all others should be guarded against scratching. Do not lean the rod against the wall of the cabin or put it in a place where it will fall over from the wind and be walked on or driven over. Hang it from a string tied to a nail or lay it down in a dry place away from traffic.

When it comes time to go home, detach the snap swivel, put it in its container in the tackle box, rewind the line onto the reel and place the end in the slot in the reel so that the line will not unwind and tangle. If this slot is not built into your reel, use an elastic band, kept on the reel for this purpose, and merely wrap the band over the line end as it is wound on the spool.

To break the rod down, gently pull the sections straight apart. Do not twist. Clean off each of the sections, remove the reel and place the rod in the case and reel in the box. Now all is ready for the next fishing trip.

RECOMMENDED SPINNING TACKLE FOR AVERAGE FRESHWATER FISHING

This is the very general rule of thumb to follow in tackle selection. Rod action—the variation from stiff tip to soft-action tip—makes a great deal of difference in the handling of all lure weights. A stiff-tipped rod is needed to cast very heavy plugs and spoons into the wind and also to strike hard on big fish and enable the angler to drag the fish through the weeds when necessary. For most open-water fishing, and especially in quiet rivers, the light gear will be most suitable. For fast trout-stream work, where the fish congregate in the rips, a slightly heavier tip and stronger line is advised even when fishing with light lures.

FISH SIZE	REEL	ROD	LINE	LURE WEIGHTS
small trout, panfish, bass, short casts	ultralight–light	ultralight 5 to 6 ft.	4, 6 lbs.	$\frac{1}{8}$ to $\frac{3}{8}$ oz.
medium casts	light–medium action	6 to 6½ ft.	6, 8 lbs.	$\frac{1}{4}$ to $\frac{1}{2}$ oz.
big bass, pike, heavyweight, hard conditions	medium–heavy	6½ to 7½ ft.	10 lbs.	$\frac{1}{2}$ to 1 oz. or heavier

2 BAIT CASTING

BAIT-CASTING ROD

The bait-casting rod and reel are as old as fishing itself. The reel action is based on the barrel or line spool revolving and feeding the line off or taking it back on as the spool is turned by a handle. The modern multiplying reel spool turns about four revolutions to one turn of the handle. The first reel spools turned only as the handle itself was turned. A level-wind mechanism in the form of a frame on a crossbar was added as a refinement so that the line would be reeled onto the spool evenly (see Fig. 2-1).

The first bait-casting rods made of split bamboo, steel and finally glass, both solid and tubular, had straight handles upon which the reel was mounted. In order to make the line control easier, the offset handle was invented to set the reel in easier position, and the line is fed through the guides that are also mounted on the top side of the rod (see Fig. 2-2).

In the early days lines were made of braided silk, but today braided nylon has become the accepted line to use. For special instances, the monofilament line is also used, and this will be detailed later.

Rod Grip

As you can see from Fig. 2-3, showing the typical offset-handled rod with the bait-casting reel mounted on the top, the handle is free to grasp easily with your thumb resting on the top. Do not turn your hand so that you can see your fingernails. The trigger on the bottom of the rod handle just under the reel is there for your forefinger to use as a pressure and fulcrum point

FIGURE 2-1. LEVEL-WIND MECHANISM ON
BAIT-CASTING REEL

This is the bar that moves back and forth
across the reel to distribute the line evenly
on the spool when it is being retrieved. As
the cast is made, the line also flows through
the level-wind bars for even casting tension.

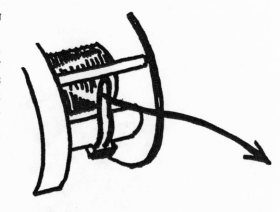

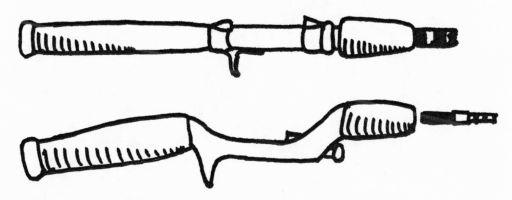

FIGURE 2-2. STRAIGHT AND OFFSET HANDLES

On top is the straight-handled rod
inherited from many years of tackle
development and still preferred by many
anglers. On the bottom is the offset handle
which allows a lower position for the reel
and a better and easier thumb position on
the line.

FIGURE 2-3. HAND POSITION: BAIT-CASTING
REEL

This is the manner of holding the bait-
casting rod for casting. Note that the
thumb falls conveniently on the line spool
for instant and constant control. The grip
should be easy, relaxed and soft. There is
no need for grip tension. Save that energy
for the cast and its control.

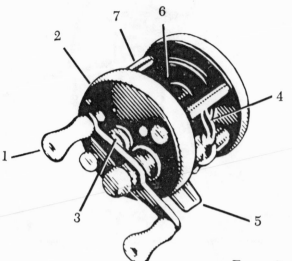

FIGURE 2–4. BAIT-CASTING REEL

This is a typical bait-casting reel complete with the level-wind mechanism and drag. The parts as labeled include: 1] Handle or crank. 2] Head. 3] Drag. 4] Level wind. 5] Cross plate or foot. 6] Spool. 7] Pillar.

in casting. The thumb rests naturally on the reel spool and touches the line as it should for control during the cast. That's all there is to it.

There is a drag-control button on most reels in the center of the outside of the spool (see Fig. 2–4). For initial practice sessions it is suggested that you tighten the drag just a bit so that the spool is not running too freely. Later, after you become accustomed to the reel and its actions and your routines, you can gradually relax the drag. One of the reasons why that drag is there is for trolling purposes. When the rod is left loose in the boat and the drag is set under the pound test of the line, and a fish hits, the line will not release because the line is being trolled.

On the bait-casting rod note that the guides are much smaller than on the spinning rod, simply because the line is fed directly to the guide rather than in a loop. The reel is mounted on the top of the rod in this case, the line fed through the level-wind posts and threaded directly into the first line guide and through to the tip.

There are two types of rod handles: the straight and the offset. The straight has the reel mounted high on the handle, making it awkward for most people to easily thumb the reel and still keep the thumb in a relaxed position. The offset handle eliminates this problem for most of us.

Bait-casting rods come in either a single section or two pieces. The former is more awkward to pack and travel with, but its action is superior to the two-piece since the ferrule joint interferes a bit with the action. On some rods there is a keeper ring mounted just ahead of the handle. If there is not, hook your lure in the reel bar, not in the line guides, since this will scratch them and ruin your line.

BAIT-CASTING PROCEDURE

The essential difference between spin casting and bait casting involves the operation of the reel and the line control. Otherwise, the casting actions are exactly the same as illustrated in the chapter on spin casting.

Remember, with the spinning rod, the casting was done with the right hand and the cranking of the reel with the left hand. This required no shift of the rod in your hands. The bait-casting reel is mounted so that the handle is on the right, which means that after the cast is made, the rod and reel are quickly shifted to the left hand, and the reeling is done with the right hand.

The most important and most difficult part of learning to bait cast without a backlash in the line on the reel is the control of the line under the pressure of the cast. With the rod, reel and line set up to cast (as in spin casting, with the line and lure hanging down from the rod tip about six inches), the thumb of the casting (right) hand is placed gently on the line spool to keep it from being forced to revolve by the weight of the lure. Lift the thumb away from the spool of line, and the weight of the lure will pull off line and cause the reel spool to revolve. If you do not stop it from revolving at that instant, when the lure hits the floor, the reel spool will keep on revolving, even though the line is not being pulled off. That is what is known as a backlash. This is just a small example of what can happen during a power cast, forcing you to take off a half hour to get the line untangled.

To avoid all this, start easily, feeling your way and getting used to the release of the line to allow the lure to fall to the floor.

Stop the spool the instant the lure hits the floor and you will not have an overlap on the spool. Try this several times before you attempt to cast.

Now vibrate the rod tip, holding your thumb on the line with more pressure, since the lure will exert pull on the line. On one of the downward thrusts release the line under the thumb for an instant and then snub it again. The lure moved out from the rod tip in a simulated cast. If your timing was right, there is no backlash there, under your thumb.

The Retrieve

The best habit to get into is, after switching the rod from the right hand to the left, to slide the left hand forward of the reel, grasp the incoming line in your thumb and forefinger, and set a slight tension as the line is retrieved (see Fig. 2–5). This helps to keep the line clean and to feed line onto the reel under equal pressure so that it will cast evenly the next time. Practice this hand switching and the assuming of this hand-forward position a few times until it becomes second nature. It is seldom advisable to reel in the line unguided.

In this position, you control the angle of the rod as well, vibrating the rod up and down or sideways to manipulate your lure on the retrieve. The right hand does the cranking.

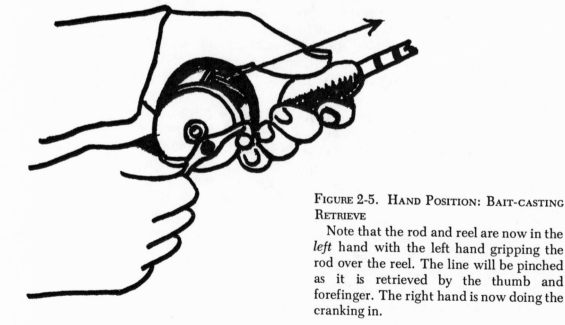

FIGURE 2-5. HAND POSITION: BAIT-CASTING RETRIEVE

Note that the rod and reel are now in the *left* hand with the left hand gripping the rod over the reel. The line will be pinched as it is retrieved by the thumb and forefinger. The right hand is now doing the cranking in.

To actually make a cast, proceed slowly as you did in the spin-casting sequence. From now on the efforts are exactly the same and the results are the same. Make sure you train that thumb to be ultrasensitive.

Putting your tackle away temporarily or packing it away until the next trip is done in the same sequence you performed in spinning. Care for your tackle, baby it, and it will serve you well!

You may decide, after reading these directions, to skip bait casting altogether. Actually, bait casting is more detailed and requires more fussing than spin casting, but it is a popular method. I prefer to use the bait-casting rod when I want to troll, but trolling can be done as well with the spinning gear. Even for the heaviest of fish, such as the pike and muskellunge, I use spinning gear in the appropriate weight and balance. I prefer to spin, simply because I'm lazy and don't like the nerve strain of possible backlashes.

Striking, Playing, Landing

Striking, playing and landing the fish with bait-casting tackle is very similar to that of spinning, except that your thumb is still the final authority over the line on the strike, during the playing and at the time of netting the fish. Seldom will you play the fish from the reel unless it is a very large one on a particularly fast run. Then the reel drag, preset under the breaking strain of the line, takes over. You maintain the line control with the rod in the left hand, with your thumb on the spool controlling the line. The right hand is there on the handle to bring in the line and maintain the pressure on the fish. The striking and playing positions are shown in the chapter on fly-fishing and indicate just how dangerous the down position is. Keep that rod up.

3 FLY-FISHING

LEARNING TO SET UP GEAR

In fly-fishing the synchronization of rod, reel, line and line handling is more difficult to learn at first than the other two methods. It is the most subtle of the three, demanding a relaxed, though accurate feel of the balanced tackle in motion. It is a delight to perform as well as to watch. Great things can happen in fly-fishing, and its mastery is the true art of fishing.

The fly rod is the longest of the three, and this length is required in order to make the line perform properly in the air and on the cast (see Fig. 3-1). The lure, a very light fly in comparison to the lures used in bait and spin fishing, merely goes along for the ride. Its weight does not pull the line from the reel. Actually the line and leader can be cast without a fly on the end. The reel is mounted behind the hand and hangs down, in contrast to the spinning and bait-casting reels that are mounted ahead of the hand or, in the case of the open-face spinning reel, straddled by the fingers in the center of the rod handle. The rod guides are small in diameter, since the line is fed directly to the guides from the hand, not generally from the reel.

The reel itself is merely a spool to keep the line (see Fig. 3-2). The fish is seldom if ever played from the reel with the exception of very big trout or salmon. It is of single action, non-multiplying, and in most cases, requires no drag mechanism, except for playing the very biggest fish. This control is mainly used to keep the line from ripping off the reel too fast.

The lines come in various sizes and tapers as is shown in Fig. 3-3. These tapers have very definite purpose and function in the various uses they are put to.

FIGURE 3–1. FLY-FISHING TACKLE

This is the conventional fly-fishing outfit of rod, reel, line and leader as it is set to go with the fly hooked into the fly keeper ring. The leader is tied onto the line as directed in the chapter on terminal tackle. Note that the reel is in the "down" position and is seldom used in the upright position. The guides are very small, since the line is fed directly except for the first guide which is usually round and a trifle larger than the "snake" guides farther out. Illustrated is the preferred two-piece rod, though it is a bit long for easy carrying and travel. Rods also come in three sections. Setting the rod up and being careful with the jointing and unjointing is as important as it is in bait- and spin-casting tackle to keep the rod unscratched, unbent and always in perfect condition. The handle is of cork. The reel seat is either a keeper ring that slides over the base of the reel or a screw type. The screw type is preferred so that the reel is not accidentally dropped. Rod material is either tubular glass or split bamboo. Glass is recommended for the beginner. Good bamboo rods are quite expensive and really unnecessary until you reach the point of fastidious desires in rod action.

FIGURE 3–2. FLY-FISHING REELS

The single-action fly reel is used mainly for carrying the line only. Seldom is the fish played from the reel, since the control of the line is by the line hand in all cases except when playing big fish such as steelhead and salmon. The large size balances with large rods and is used because it affords spool space for a large amount of level braided "running" line which is tied into the tapered line. The automatic reel operates to retrieve the line by the mere pressing of a lever, eliminating the long procedure of stripping in the line by hand. The fish can also be played by the reel pressure in this case when desired.

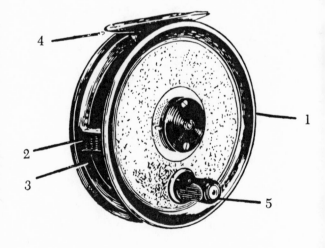

The reel shown here illustrates the following parts: 1] Detachable spool. 2] Crossbar. 3] Line guide. 4] Foot. 5] Handle. (Some reels also have built-in drag adjustment.)

FIGURE 3-3. FLY-ROD LINES

These are the three types of fly lines: level, double-tapered and weight-forward "bullet" or "fast-taper" lines.

1] The level line is used mainly for very short casts with a six-foot leader and weightless or weighted hook for bait or flies. It will not cast far.

2] This is the double taper—a flat running line, a taper to a designated thickness that again tapers off toward the end with a short length of level line before the leader. Tapered leaders of from six to nine feet are used with this for wet and dry fly-fishing. This line will cast forty to fifty feet with the average rod when you are using light flies and very small weightless bait.

3] This is the weight-forward line taper. It is used for distance work using small flies or a single fly. The reason this type of line is recommended is that the long running line behind the taper remains on the reel while you are false-casting to gain power in the cast. A very short and quick taper, this is the only part of the line that is in the air during the false cast. The weight here will carry the running line out as you will see when I detail this process later.

The variations in all these lines for specific weights of rod is shown on p. 30 in rod and line recommendations.

There are two basic types of fly lines—the *floating* and the *sinking*. The floating is used for dry fly-fishing when it is desirable for the line to float, and the sinking for wet fly-fishing if it is desired that the line sink.

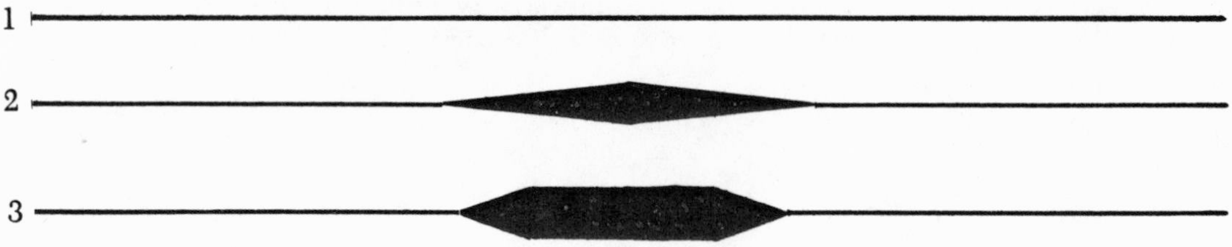

In the torpedo, bullet or weight-forward lines (30 yards long) the American Fishing Tackle Manufacturer's Association (AFTMA) designations and alphabetical designations are:

Floating	Sinking
GAAF—9	GAF—8
GAF—8	GBF—7
GBF—7	HCF—6
HCF—6	HDG—5
HDG—5	

In the double taper (30 yards long):

Floating	Sinking
GBG—7	GBG—7
HCH—6	HCH—6
HDH—5	HDH—5
HEH—4	HEH—4

In the level lines (25 yards long):

Floating	Sinking
B—7	B—7
C—6	C—6
D—5	D—5
E—4	E—4
F—3	

Leaders, attached to the end of the line, are also tapered in most cases to balance the end of the cast and set the fly properly on the water. They are also tapered as thinly as possible to allow freedom of movement to the fly and less visibility to the fish. Thus, the fly appears to be a natural thing, not something attached to a line. See Fig. 3–4.

Fly-rod action is another consideration when balancing fly-fishing tackle for casting. The setups in the following table are those used by many experts and they seem to cover all basic needs well. The heavy combination is used frequently in salmon fishing when extra distance is needed as in a stiff wind and where heavy flies are in order. Glass is preferred, although the specialist can obtain specially tapered bamboo rods for specific

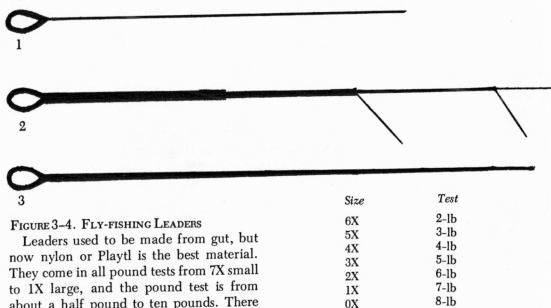

FIGURE 3–4. FLY-FISHING LEADERS

Size	Test
6X	2-lb
5X	3-lb
4X	4-lb
3X	5-lb
2X	6-lb
1X	7-lb
0X	8-lb

Leaders used to be made from gut, but now nylon or Playtl is the best material. They come in all pound tests from 7X small to 1X large, and the pound test is from about a half pound to ten pounds. There are both level leaders and tapered. The tapered leaders are made from taking stepped-down sections of leader and tying them together, or you can buy tapered leaders of nylon that are manufactured or "drawn" in specific tapers. If it is desired to taper a drawn leader further "up" or "down," sections can be added by tying the desired strands in.

One manufacturer's sample lists the Playtl tapered leaders as follows:

These leaders (in both 7½- and 9½-foot lengths) are color keyed and come packaged in see-through envelopes, in a book. Each size leader is tinted a different color for quick identification so that there is no excuse for having the wrong one.

Leaders pictured in the diagram are: *1]* Level leader and loop; *2]* leader tapered by sections; *3]* drawn-tapered one-piece leader.

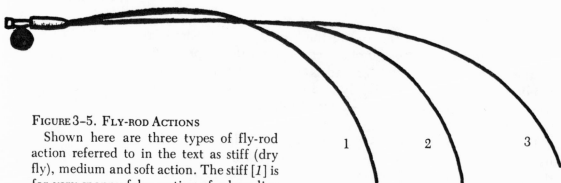

FIGURE 3–5. FLY-ROD ACTIONS

Shown here are three types of fly-rod action referred to in the text as stiff (dry fly), medium and soft action. The stiff [1] is for very snappy false casting of a long line and the casting of a dry fly. In the case of the bass-bug rod, specifically designed to throw the heavier, wind-resistant bugs, a long, nine-and-a-half footer is needed in this action. Some stiff-action dry fly rods are only six feet long. The medium action [2] is for both shorter-length dry fly casting and wet fly-fishing with one or two flies.

The soft action [3] is for shorter dry fly-fishing, wet fly and nymph fishing and very light baits. Tapered lines to fit are shown in the table of recommendations for balanced tackle. If the line does not fit the rod, it will not cast well, so balanced rod and line is a must.

Recommended balanced rods, reels, lines and leaders for specific combinations for typical fishing requirements

FISHING TYPE	ROD LENGTH (medium action)	REEL	LINE TAPER	LEADER SIZE
Panfish, small trout and bass	7ft.	Small	HDH	Tap to 4X
Medium trout, bass longer casts	8 ft.	Medium	HCH	Tap to 3X
Heavy trout and bass	8½ ft.	Large	GAF	Tap to 3X or 2X
Bass bug, salmon	9½ ft.	Large	G2AF	Tap to 2X

demands. All actions specified here are medium. The stiff-action rods are preferred if the angler is going to do a great deal of dry fly-fishing. Fig. 3–5 illustrates the various fly-rod actions.

I have devised a very simple explanation in words and diagrams to show how easy the procedure of casting can be. I have learned, by teaching hundreds of anglers to cast in but a few moments, that when they get the visual concept of what the line does in the air, they can quickly master the actions of fly-fishing.

In bait casting and spin casting, the lure was the object which pulled the line from the reel on the cast. In fly-fishing, the line does all the work, and the fly, as we have said, goes along for the ride. In order to bring this about, the rod is cast or waved in much the same way as the others. The line control, however, is an important part of the casting and is controlled by the left (free) hand.

To assemble the gear, place the fly rod on the handle so that the reel faces down and the line on the reel coils off from the bottom of the reel toward the first guide. Secure the reel well. If the handle has a ring, press this against the reel foot tightly. If the screw-locking reel seat is present on your rod, secure the reel firmly in place. Thread the line through the first guide. Now insert the second section of the rod, lining up the guides before you insert so as not to twist the ferrule joints. Thread the line through these guides to the next section or tip-top, if you are using only a two-piece rod. With the line extending from the rod tip, attach the leader loop with the line-to-leader knot as shown in Chapter 4 on terminal tackle.

It is best to introduce you to fly casting without using a fly. While it is best to do this practice over water, a snag-free lawn will do very nicely. Do not cast the line over sand, concrete or gravel, since the finish is not made to stand this friction and roughness.

LEARNING TO MAKE THE CASTS

Rod Grip

As you can see from the diagram of a typical setup in Fig. 3–6, the handle of the rod is ahead of the reel. Your grip then has nothing to do with the reel whatsoever. All you do is cast the rod with the right hand. The reel is tended with the other hand.

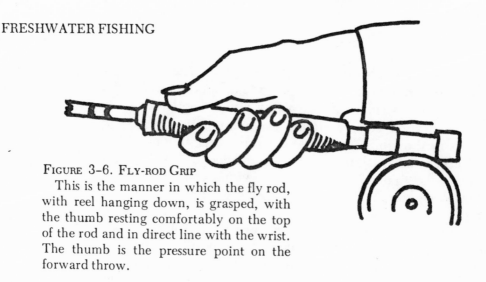

FIGURE 3-6. FLY-ROD GRIP

This is the manner in which the fly rod, with reel hanging down, is grasped, with the thumb resting comfortably on the top of the rod and in direct line with the wrist. The thumb is the pressure point on the forward throw.

Grasp the rod so that your thumb rests easily on top of the handle. Seldom, except when resting, is the hand turned so that the back of the hand is on top. The main pressure point in the cast, particularly the forward part of the cast, is the thumb, which exerts the pressure here. With the thumb on top, the wrist will not have the tendency to break, thereby allowing the rod to go too far back from the vertical position in the peak of the cast. Again, do not grasp the rod handle too tightly. Be relaxed about it or you will tend to tense up and tire quickly.

FIGURE 3-7. STEPS IN THE CASTING

These are the steps in making the simple fore-and-aft cast with the fly tackle. Note how the line acts in the air from the various pressures. Notice, as in spin and bait casting, that the entire motion is conducted, during the short and usually effortless cast, by the hand and wrist only (the arm will be used on the power casts and when more distance and direction power is used). The hand in this instance is the fulcrum of power and directs all energy which is transferred to the rod. In this casting, the rod does practically all the work for you. Don't get into the habit of unneeded pressure. Allow the rod to perform its function *for* you, since all you need to do is to guide it and apply pressure as needed.

Starting at the pickup, [1] in diagram A, through to [2], you exert an upward snaplike pressure, and at [2] the action literally stops for a split second and the rod does all the performing, bending as shown in a backward direction. This timing allows the line to sail out behind and above you. At the instant the line straightens out—you'll get to "feel" this as you progress—you pressure forward sharply. DO NOT LET THE HAND FLIP OVER BACKWARD BEYOND THE VERTICAL. If you do, the rod will go too far back, lose its power, and the line will fall too low.

Diagram B shows the forward part of the cast, almost identical to diagram A, but in reverse. To maintain the false cast, do not allow the rod to fall to position [2] (it is shown here only to illustrate the completed cast).

Diagram C shows the entire cast from beginning to end, with the final drop down. Note again that the forearm and arm are stationary throughout.

A

B

C

I will demonstrate the cast for you, so that you can see what happens. This will give your mind's eye the picture, and then you can, with instruction, duplicate it. The first principle is that the line, to be cast well and accurately, must travel straight out behind you and remain high in the air or it will not cast straight out in front of you. To accomplish this, an equalized pressure of fore and aft cast is made from the pickup point, to the vertical pause, through the forward throw and the letdown. See Figs. 3–7 and 3–8.

FIGURE 3-8. WRIST AND ARM MOTION IN CONCERT WITH LINE STRIPPING

Here you see the more powerful cast, which uses the forearm and, actually, the entire arm, in concert with the line stripping done by the "line" (i.e., left) hand and arm. While this seems to be complicated at first look, you'll get the feeling of the sequences readily with some practice. After a few casts, it will become almost second nature.

Before, only the hand was turned from horizontal to vertical position. Now, the forearm and arm are introduced into the picture for added power and more direction control (in the instance where you wish to change direction of the cast to the right or left). Note the sequence and make the cast *without any line stripping*, as you did during your first cast.

1] pickup

2] upward pressure
3] vertical pause
4] forward push
5] downward fall

Then, to maintain the false cast, do not go to position [5] or the drop, but proceed through the pickup and continue the routine, bringing the forearm and full arm into the "swing" for the added power you'll need later. This is done with the short line now, but will, as we extend the line, be needed to maintain the power and smoothness of the cast.

Line stripping is basically two actions: the stripping of line from the reel on the backward part of the cast and the letting out of the line on the forward part of the cast. You maintain the cast with the additional line by exerting more pressure to send the longer line on its way.

I have performed this cast using a short line of about twenty feet with only the casting arm, just to give you the idea of the rhythm of the cast and the direction of the line in the air. To reach out further, I must use the left (line) hand for additional control and for retrieving the line for the next cast. I'm using a double-tapered line which is not a *shooting* line, a cast that I will go into later. For now, the HDH double-tapered line on the medium-action rod of seven and a half feet will show you the basics.

Note, as I cast again, that I can cast this length of line quickly with the possibility of a snap of the leader end as the leader whips out in back and out in front. As the line goes back and forth (this is known as the *false cast*), the line is not being allowed to settle on the water in front as it does in the legitimate cast. The reason for the false cast is to gain balance in the air and direction of the line so that the fly lets down on the water gently. Notice that when you learn to false-cast the line in the air, you can vary the pressure and speed, still keeping the line going out-and-back, out-and-front with ease. Adjust your casting pressure so that the line does not drop down behind you but stays well up off the water, away from rocks and snags. Try this with twenty feet of line measured from the rod tip. After getting used to this, you can work with a longer line.

To lengthen the line, grasp the line between the reel and the first guide. As you begin the cast by lifting the line off the water, pull or strip off line from the reel, making the back cast as usual, and on the forward throw, release the line that you stripped from the reel, keeping hold of the line when it stops slipping through your fingers.

Now make the false cast out back again and note that the extra line is felt as additional pressure. A slightly longer pause is necessary at the top, and a quicker forward motion is required, since the added line will tend to drop more quickly. Now strip off another couple of feet of line as before. As you draw back for the next false cast, strip off line from the reel, and as you come forward release the line through your fingers, still keeping control. As the line straightens out, pull back before it begins to drop, using a bit more power. Strip off more line now as it is coming back and, on the forward throw, allow the line to slip through the fingers. By now you are false-casting nearly thirty feet of line evenly in the air. Keep it up by varying your pressures. Then, on one of the forward throws, when you feel comfortable and the line is balanced in the air, allow the line to drop down in front of you. See? You have just made your first cast, and it is well-nigh perfect!

Essentially, that is all there is to fly casting in the common, fore-and-aft cast. The rest is refinement—equalizing the pressures of the line and rod action, of the rod handle and the line hand on the line.

To begin again, it is not advisable to try and lift all that line from the water to make another cast. So you strip in line. Hold the rod in position at about two o'clock and, grasping the line near the first guide, strip down by pulling in line, three times at about two feet at a time (the amount you used in your extensions before).

You are now ready to lift the line off the water to begin the false cast again. Pick up by first lowering the rod tip from the old position, lifting up sharply and swinging the rod to the vertical position. Continue this back and forth in the false cast just as you started some minutes ago. When your line is casting in the air back and forth easily, you can again lengthen the line, adjust the timing and pressure of the cast and extend the line even farther than you did the last time. Note that a slower timing is needed as the line extends out and more pressure is needed to keep the line up off the water in the back cast and forward cast. Let it down again. See how that leader lies down on the water with hardly a ripple.

VARIATIONS ON THE FORE-AND-AFT CAST

Some variations are worth noting at this early stage in your casting. If you wish to change the direction of the cast, you can do so during the false cast by gradually changing your point of aim more toward the left or right of center. You can also do this by making the cast from a slight angle from the vertical position, leaning the rod to the left or right as your choice dictates.

The same cast can be made horizontally over the water. This is tricky, since you have so little space to drop down to the water and the speed of the cast must be much faster. This cast is used when casting to a target under overhangs or when casting into a very stiff wind.

If you are casting to a rock above you in the stream (see Fig. 3-9) and you wish to cast with a bend in the leader section, either to the left or the right, turn your hand in the direction needed on the forward throw and then, just before the line

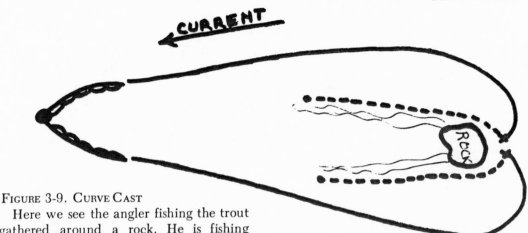

FIGURE 3-9. CURVE CAST

Here we see the angler fishing the trout gathered around a rock. He is fishing upstream from a downstream position and casts so that his line falls above and partially around the rock for a good drift over the hot spots. The broken line shows the line and fly drifting down to the pickup point for the recast. This is a valuable cast, especially when fishing along a bank or trying to float a line in under an overhanging rock or tree branch or snag.

touches the water on the drop, come up sharply about ten degrees on the rod. This hand roll will whip the end of the leader in the desired direction. A little practice and the line will fall like this on the water. Fig. 3-10 demonstrates a casting variation.

Shooting the Line

Armed now with a powerful and long fly rod with a stiff tip section, a weight-forward tapered line, tapered leader and a small fly, I can demonstrate the great distances you can cast with the fly-fishing method.

Since all the weight of the line is located in the first few yards, it is difficult to cast this length of line in the air in the usual false cast. In order to build up casting power in the rod, wave it back and forth and make a short false cast with only about half the taper out from the rod tip. This heavy weight in the air, being pushed back and forth by the stiff rod, will build up the tension needed to shoot the line forward. The cast is begun just as is the fore-and-aft false cast. As you are performing this, strip off several coils of line. (At first you might drop the line at your feet for practice sake.) When you choose to release the line for the forward drop, the weight of the line combined with the power of the cast will rapidly pick up all that line and even strain the reel for more. So give it more! Strip off more line for the next cast. You'll find, when you learn the tricky timing, that you can shoot as much as thirty feet of line. Add this to the thirty feet of line already in the air and you are reaching out almost to the sixty-foot mark. That little dry fly on the end is really going for a ride.

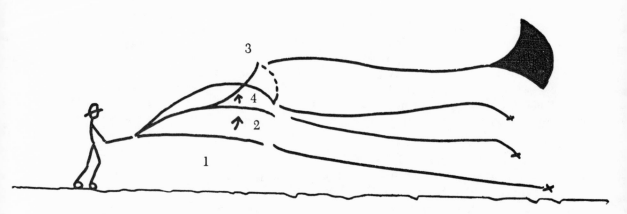

FIGURE 3-10. ROLL-PICKUP CAST

This is seldom seen performed by the average angler, yet it is a very simple and necessary part of the casting of the line and of the better fishing techniques.

Do it this way. Your fly is out there lying on the water—in slack water for this instance so there is no hurry in the learning of the process.

Begin as you would in the ordinary pickup of the cast for the conventional fore-and-aft cast. Almost after you have started the pickup, you very forcefully snap the rod down again, which pulls the fly and end of the leader off the water. Almost as quickly as you did the first two moves, and as the fly leaves the water, pull back harder than usual on the regular cast and then begin your conventional false cast. Now go through this again. The line and fly are on the water. Snap a sharp pickup motion and

at the same time, snap the rod down again. As the fly comes out as a result of this action on the line, pull back hard and perform your regular false cast. Note how little line disturbance you caused. Just for contrast, put the line and fly out there on the water again and, in one motion, begin to pull it all back to start the regular cast. See what a strip of water was disturbed? In order to get more power in this roll pickup, especially if you are fishing upstream against a current dragging the fly down toward you, strip in line at the instant you begin the pickup and forward flip. This will make sure the line acts as it should in preparation to the false-cast position.

Try this a few times, and you'll find it an easy task.

The roll cast in Fig. 3-11 is simply a powerful version of the same cast, but with a different purpose.

To further help the cast and give it more power, you perform what is known as the *power cast* or *double haul.* As you begin the pickup off the water, or the backward swing from the front false-cast position, grasp the line near the first guide and pull it in with a sharp downward pull. As the line flies backward to the back position of the false cast, release the line you have taken in. Then as it begins to fly forward, pull line in again from the first guide and release it. In this way, you are amplifying the power of the rod through the restriction of the line during the cast.

Line Retrieve in Upstream Fishing

"This is all well and good. I can make the cast," you may say. "But what is happening as I am fishing upstream and that line is drifting down upon me with great bends of slack. I'll be in a tangle."

Well, in addition to the casting, upstream fishing also requires a constant retrieve of the line with the left hand while you are casting with the right. Right after the upstream cast is made, begin to strip line in. Don't pull too fast or you'll pull the fly that is supposed to drift by itself down to you. In stripping the line on a fairly short cast, it is all right to allow the slack line to slip through your fingers and drift below you. On very long casts, it is better to coil the line in your hand, since you will be needing it to feed out from the reel again as you did in your first steps. You no longer deal with the reel, under this circumstance, but deal with the line that is floating behind you or coiled in your hand. For all intents and purposes, you are now the reel.

In across-stream and across-and-downstream fishing, the problem is not as difficult as in direct upstream fishing. Here the line can be allowed to float below you without tangling. But if you are using a very long line, again you must coil it in your hand.

The roll pickup is a refinement of the pickup which can and should be used almost all the time for easy fishing; it is an effortless pickup that does not disturb the water very much.

Roll Cast

This cast is fully as important to the well-rounded angler as the fore-and-aft cast. In fact, many anglers use it almost exclusively under certain conditons. Basically it is used when there is no room for the backswing of the conventional cast. If you are

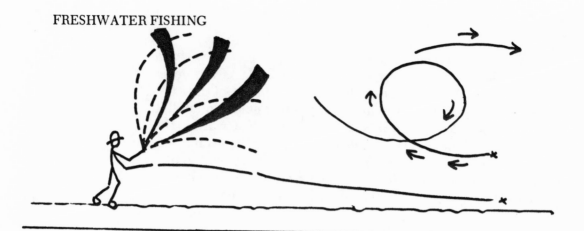

FIGURE 3-11. ROLL CAST

This is what the cast actually looks like in stop motion. Almost as this is started, the line comes up off the water in similar fashion to the roll pickup, which you have already performed, and looks like the big circle in the diagram. As usual in these diagrams, the X denotes the fly. Note that the loop is formed as a result of the double pressures on the rod. The fly loops toward your face, and up in front of you, curving away from you straight out but high in the air to go into the final drop-down position.

This is how it looks. Now let's perform it step-by-step in Fig. 3-12.

FIGURE 3-12. ROLL CAST

In the A section of the diagram, the first part of the cast is executed. Starting with the line in the in-stream position [1], ready for the pickup, the rod is jerked strongly into the vertical position, all in one quick motion. Just as the hand, wrist and arm assume this position, the line moves in toward you as shown [2], preparatory to its wide, high, circular pattern in the form of a loop (as shown in diagram B).

Now, in diagram B, at position [2], the forward pressure is exerted toward position [3] and the line continues to pass near you on its upward swing to form the loop which develops as you bring down the rod to position [4]. When your rod comes down to position [5], the line is now on its way out toward the target, and at [6] the line falls to the target area. The whole thing is really a *snap* (pun intended!). Snap up and then, quickly, down again, and the whole routine performs by itself.

Once again now. Start with the line out, bring the rod up sharply to the vertical and just as sharply down again. The line reacts to all this by coming close to you and forming a forward loop to straighten out in the air above the target and then fall to the water. Fascinating to watch, fun to perform, you'll use this cast a great deal, in your stream fishing especially. As usual, try this cast with a short line at first to get the routines set in your head. Then you can extend the line length. Actually, when you want to learn to extend the line on this cast, all you do is feed extra line when position [5] is in effect on the forward swing. You have drawn it out from the reel preparatory to the cast. To add more power and zip to the cast, as you begin the pickup, strip in line from the first guide and pull down hard as you begin the cast to the vertical position.

40

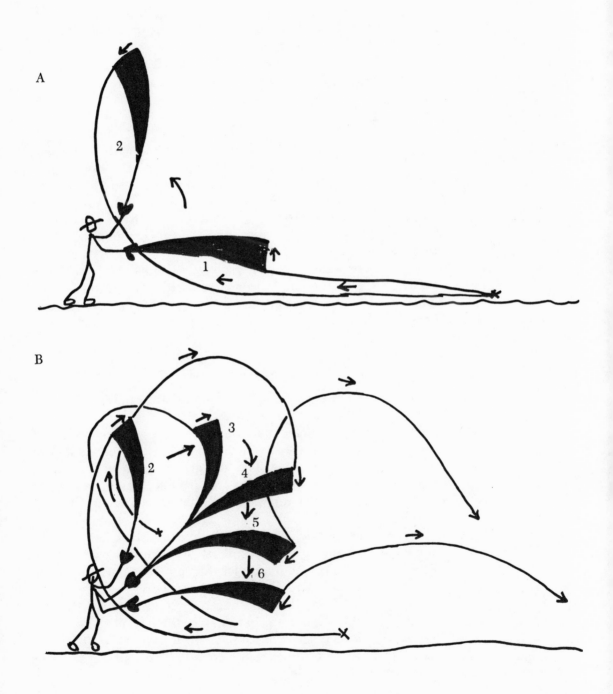

fishing with brush and trees or a bridge or cliff behind you, you cannot perform the usual cast, so you use the roll cast.

At other times, you do not need to bother with the conventional cast—for instance, when you are fishing down and across stream and only wish to flip the flies out into the current a short distance. You'll find hundreds of instances where you'll use the roll cast rather than the fore-and-aft.

Study the diagrams in Figs. 3–11 and 3–12 and perform the cast by the steps indicated in the captions.

Roll-and-Mend Cast

The roll-and-mend cast is used when you wish to change direction in roll casting or combine the roll with the fore-and-aft cast. Suppose you are casting straight out from you and wish to bring the line upstream or, in this case, to the left. You simply swing the rod angled to the upstream or left direction, and the line will bend in this direction and then shoot out to the left. Reverse the action to mend to the right.

With these casts you are ready to fish. When you have mastered them, you can be concerned with presentation of the lures in the currents and the striking, playing and landing operation once you have that fish on the hook.

STRIKING, PLAYING AND LANDING

This is the action part of the tackle handling and is equally as important as the casting and line retrieve.

In fly casting, the left (line) arm does most of the controlling of the action, and the fish is not played from the reel as it is in spinning and bait casting. The line arm (except when playing big steelhead or Atlantic salmon) does all the controlling in conjunction with the rod pressure that is exerted by the rod hand.

If the fish strikes when there is little or no slack line lying on the water or hanging loosely underwater, the strike will be felt immediately. Your reaction under this condition must not be too abrupt or strong. Actually, when this occurs, the fish usually hooks himself! It is when the line is slack that more attention must be paid to taking up that slack at the instant the fish hits. Otherwise, if there is too much slack, he'll have time to taste and reject the lure in one quick split second. Try to control your slack line as much as possible.

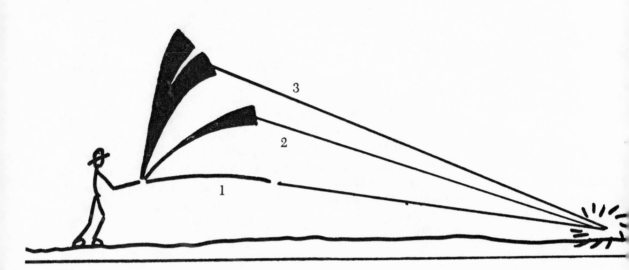

FIGURE 3-13. STRIKING, PLAYING, LANDING

Here you see yourself at the instant a fish strikes, or during the playing of the fish. If you were to have the rod in the down or [1] position, the line would be directly pointed at the fish and subject to breaking if the fish pulled with more pressure than the pound test of the leader. So you use the rod as the cushion. Position [2] is better, and if the fish is playing deep, this is often sufficient, though it is still not a safe position if the fish is a big one in fast and snaggy water. It is best to assume position [3] where you can exercise better control as well as possess the reserve allowance of the spring of the rod. You can, in this position, adjust the pull against the fish or the release of pressure by both lowering the rod tip slightly and at the same time giving a bit of line in combination, making sure you can gain the line back quickly by either retrieving it or pulling back on the rod or both, so that slack line does not develop. This vertical position is a must (or its corresponding horizontal position since either is almost a right angle to the line of fight).

At the time of almost landing your fish, the rod is held high and the slack line is gathered in the left hand. At convenient times during the fight, as the line is brought in, the line can be held in the rod hand while the left hand is used in reeling in slack, a necessity if the current is strong and will tangle the line or if you are fishing in brushy circumstances where the line could snag.

To net the fish, be sure that it is fully played out. If you are fishing from a wading position in a fast stream, try to get the fish upcurrent from you and then let it drop back slowly into the submerged landing net. Hold the line in the rod hand and execute the landing with the left hand, free now since the line is under control. Don't swipe at the fish, but rather merely hold the net into a position where the fish will drop back into it and then you can scoop him up, relaxing the line in the rod hand at that same instant to release the pressure from the bent rod.

43

Remember that with light fly-fishing gear, the lighter the leader the better. It will not only be less visible to the fish but will also afford a more natural movement to the fly due to its lightness and suppleness. But don't let that light test of, say, a 4X two-pound test leader, scare you. If used properly it will hold a three-pound trout or even larger bass, because the rod is more limp in action and supplies the needed cushion for the strike and also for the playing.

Get in the routine of always raising the rod tip after the cast. In this position, the full bend of the rod will be exercised when the fish strikes or when you are playing him. If the rod is held in the down position, the line is pointed at the dead center of the pressure exerted by the fish on the take or in play, and the cushion is then nonexistent. So keep that rod up, or if forced into a horizontal position, keep it well back in a right-angle position (see Fig. 3–13).

TERMINAL TACKLE 4

LURE SELECTION AND ARTIFICIAL FLIES

Artificial flies fall into two basic categories—those designed to imitate actual insects upon which the fish feed and those that are made to appear like minnows or small bait fish. Essentially they are made of feathers and bits of hair or fur tied onto a hook shank that is covered with a "body." Some are designed to float like a real insect on the water surface, others are fished below the surface in drift or active action. Various trout fly types are illustrated in Fig. 4-1.

The minnow and bait-fish imitations are mostly fished under the water, and some are weighted to make them sink even deeper. They are made in various sizes and shapes and are cast only with the fly rod. The one exception comes when fishing with the bubble and light spinning gear, which is described later in this chapter.

A special department of flies includes the bass bugs: large fluffy lures too light for bait or spin casting, but just right for specially designed fly rods. They imitate big bugs, moths, mice, frogs and the like. They float when cast and are popped and kicked across the surface of the water in a lifelike motion that attracts the fish. They are mainly used in bass fishing, although they are also quite effective on large trout at night. See Fig. 4-2.

Plastic Worms and Eels, Artificial Pork Chunk and Rind

The plastic worm and the plastic eel have all but replaced the live variety that you take from the ground. They have a lifelike

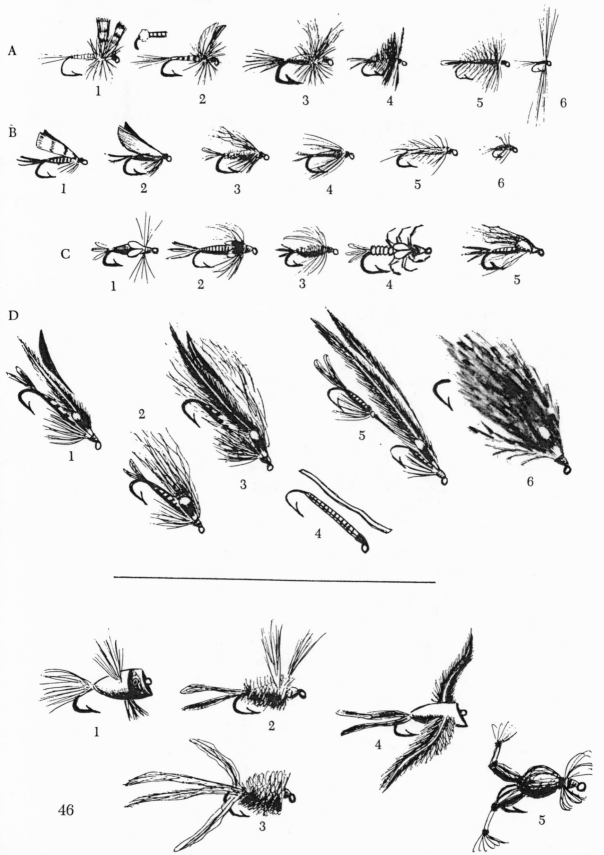

FIGURE 4-1. TROUT FLY TYPES

Shown here are the various types of flies used in trout, panfish and bass fishing in fresh water with fly-fishing tackle. As is shown later, in the section on basic terminal tackle, spinning gear can be used with flies if the plastic bubble is used in order to supply the needed weight to the cast.

Row *A* shows the dry fly types. These flies are made to imitate mayflies, caddis flies, stone flies and other aquatic insects that hatch into this flying stage in the stream and in lakes. They are made to float on the surface.

1] Divided wing type made from fibers of duck side feathers.

2] Divided wing type with sections of duck wing feathers paired to flare out.

3] Typical hair-wing fly or Wulff heavy-hook pattern particularly good for night trout fishing and Atlantic salmon fishing. It is also used for bass fishing.

4] This is the bivisible. Strands of white hackle are tied in ahead of the basic fly to make it more visible in poor light.

5] The Palmer-tied fly with the hackle tied in all the way to the hook bend. These flies sometimes have short wings as well.

6] The dainty spider fly tied on an 18 or 20 size hook. Note the long hackles.

Row *B* shows:

1] Wet version of the same above.

2] Wet version of the same above.

3] Wet version of the same above.

4] Sparsely dressed hackled fly with soft hackles so the fly will sink, not float.

5] Wet-style Palmer-like fly.

6] The wet version of the midge or spider fly.

In Row *C* are pictured:

1] Pattern of standard mayfly nymph with wing cases.

2] Longer, heavier stone-fly pattern.

3] General type of nymphlike fly.

4] Hard-bodied, exact-imitation type of plastic-molded variety.

5] Bucktaillike combination wet-nymph fly.

Row *D* illustrates:

1] Feathered streamer fly.

2] Bucktail or hair fly.

3] Weighted streamer-bucktail.

4] Strip lead, which is added to hook shank to make the weighted fly.

5] Tandem-hooked streamer fly (lake fishing for landlocked salmon).

6] Marabou.

FIGURE 4-2. BASS BUGS

Bass bugs are special creations for use with the heavy fly rod and forward-tapered line. They are supposed to represent moths, bugs, beetles, frogs, mice or anything small and fluttering on the water surface that might look like something the bass would like to eat. They are also used in big trout fishing at night on large streams, or even during the daytime when such as grasshoppers are about. They are too big a lure for panfish and pickerel, and pike do not rise to them, since these fish feed entirely on minnows and small fish. Patterns are many and specially tied bass bugs are legion. 1] Example of the wooden-bodied hair bug. 2] Entire bug made of hairs (usually deer) with long feather fiber wings. 3] Hair-bodied bug with streamer feathers. 4] Cork-, plastic- or wooden-body bug with streamer feathers. 5] Frog or mouse imitation made of long deer body hairs tied in appropriate shape to resemble either a frog or a mouse.

All these lures are made to float on the surface and be popped by rod-tip action and line manipulation.

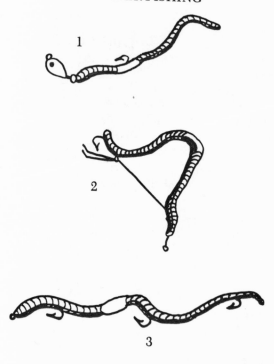

FIGURE 4-3. PLASTIC WORMS

These are available at the tackle counter in a number of basic forms as shown here. Some are available without hooks so that you can insert your own ideas for particular techniques and needs.

1] This is the metal jig with attached hook. The plastic worm is impaled on it or tied onto the hook. This is for deep-water jigging type of fishing and also for casting with a fairly fast retrieve and bounced over the bottom and through the grass.

2] This is the worm mounted on a weedless hook and attached so that the largest portion of the worm is free.

3] This shows the most deadly combination, as it is mounted with three hooks. It is either a tied-on rig or the leader is inserted into the worm and the hooks tied into the leader and reinserted into the worm. This is a good rig for casting and semistill fishing.

feel, action and color and really do the job (see Fig. 4-3). Frogs, bugs, mice and a myriad of other fish foods have been aptly imitated in plastic, looking lifelike enough to be frightening. They work! Rubber and plastic fluttering strips which resemble pork rind are also big sellers at the tackle store. The fish like them as well as the fishermen. They eliminate the mess of handling and keeping the real thing, and they work as well or better (Fig. 4-4).

Spinners and Spoons

Spoons as lures had their birth as a joke, legend tells us, when a creative fisherman cut off the spoon from its handle, attached a hook at one end and the line at the other end and cast it at the fish. When the angler retrieved the lure, it wobbled in the water enticingly and the fish struck it. From that day on, spoons in various forms, shapes, sizes and colors have been important in fishing.

The heavier spoons are used with bait-casting rigs, the lighter ones with spinning gear and the very lightest with ultralight spinning and fly tackle.

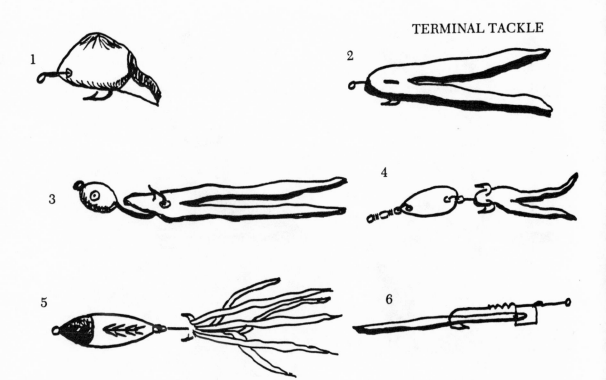

FIGURE 4-4. PORK RIND AND PORK CHUNK LURES

Bass and trout like meat. Early fishermen found this out and devised ways of cutting bits and pieces of pork (which was easily available and, in the rind, was practical since it held the hook well).

They like that same meat today as they did then. Anglers, however, always seeking ways to end the messiness of live bait or the real thing, have come up with imitations, usually made of thin rubber or plastic strips which resemble the fluttering motion of the pork rind. They are extremely effective when used in conjunction with a plug, spinner or spoon.

Shown here are a few of the types, for casting and trolling: *1*] Pork chunk on hook. *2*] Two-tail pork rind on hook. *3*] Same as [2] on a weighted jig. *4*] Strip pork on spoon (or spinner). *5*] Thin rubber (pork strips) on sinking plug. *6*] Strip-bait rig on special frame.

Spinners are merely spoons hung on a shaft that revolves instead of wobbling, giving off a different effect in the water, though it is just as deadly. They, too, come in many sizes and designs. Some spinner combinations have from two to six blades revolving on one piece of terminal tackle.

Fig. 4–5 shows some varieties of spoons and spinners.

Plugs

The term *plug* has an unknown origin. Perhaps it was a plug from a barrel with a hook attached to it that was first cast to a

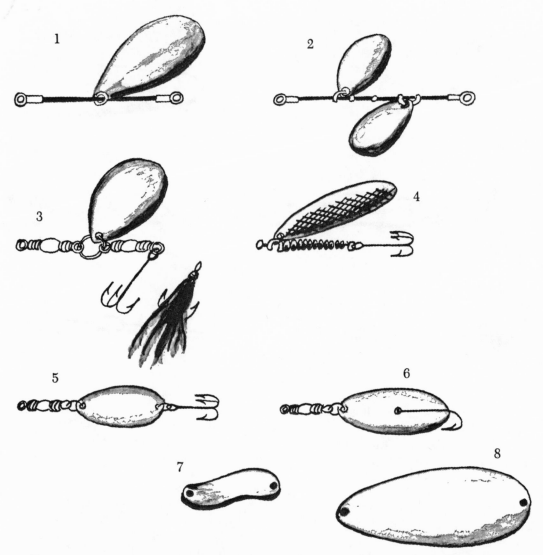

FIGURE 4-5. SPINNERS AND SPOONS

Shown here are just a few of the many variations of spinners and spoons. They are used for ultralight spinning- and fly-rod work, formal spinning and bait casting and trolling. Sometimes as many as ten spinners are employed in deep fishing, trolling spoon-spinner rigs. Spinners are often mounted ahead of a spoon, which in some opinions is the tops in deep trolling gear.

[1] is the single-bladed Indiana and [2] the double Indiana. The line is attached to one end, the hook or leader and hook to the other. [3] is the famous Colorado Spinner with the blade revolving between two swivels. It is one of the most deadly and can be used in all situations with all types of terminal tackle and fishing gear. [4] is the revolving-blade spinner ahead of the body. Good for casting and slow trolling. The typical spoon rig [5] is preceded here by the swivel and with the treble hook attached. Feathered hooks can also be used here as with others. [6] is the Johnson solid-mounted-hook spoon for trolling and casting. Good with worm bait. Finally, [7] and [8] are the original spoons just as they were made from a real spoon and handle. They can be mounted in all ways and used under all fishing conditions.

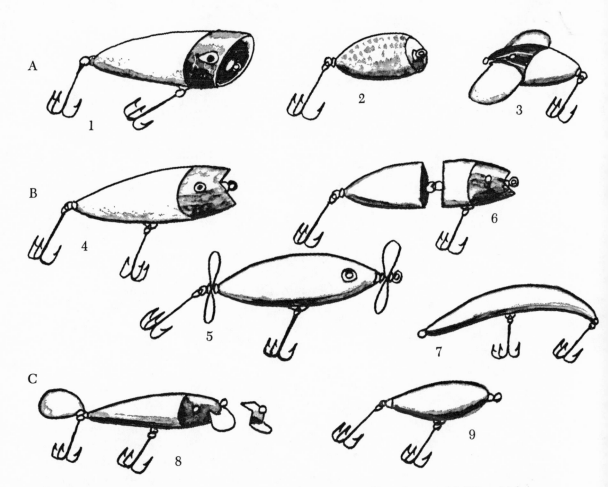

FIGURE 4-6. PLUGS

Shown here are only some of the countless shapes and forms of floating-popping, floating-diving, sinking-diving and sinking plugs. They come in all colors, particularly natural colors of bait fish such as the creek club and yellow perch. Some come with red heads, green heads, black heads and frog and minnow scales that rival the real thing.

In row A, [1] is the typical popping plug that floats when at rest. The smaller version [2] is for spinning and lighter tackle work. [3] is the popular jitterbug popping plug that comes in big sizes for heavy tackle and in several weights down to ultralight spinning size. These are all surface-acting plugs.

In row B, [4] is a typical surface-floating plug, but one that dives and zigzags the faster you pull it. Same with [6], which is a jointed model. Most of the other plugs also come jointed if you like them. [5] is one of the author's favorites, known as the fore-and-aft spinner plug which comes in either floating or sinking weight. It can be drawn across the surface or, in the sinking version, allowed to sink and then be retrieved with depth determined by the speed of retrieve. [7] is the wounded-minnow type of rolling, zigzagging plug that floats when at rest.

Row C shows the two basic types of sinking plugs (all the other versions above are also made in sinking varieties and weights). Number [8] dives at the speed of retrieve. You can also bend the front fin for further depth adjustment. Number [9] is just plain heavy with little built-in action. The action is manipulated into the lure by rod-tip motion and retrieve speed.

fish. The early inventors of plugs carved fishlike shapes from sections of broom handles, painted them and attached single, and later treble, hooks to them. These were cast on a silk line via a bait-casting rod and reel. In more recent times most of the wooden plugs have been artfully refined and balanced for all kinds of actions in the water. They are beautifully painted to represent a variety of bait fish, frogs and mice. Spinners and fins are attached for more action and attraction. Some come with fluttery skirts and feathers tied on the hooks. Plugs come in all the sizes to be used with heavy tackle as well as with the smallest of the ultralight spinning gear. Some very small plugs can be cast with the fly rod.

Plug actions fall into definite categories as is shown in Fig. 4-6. A broad selection of the illustrated types completes a basic collection of plugs.

NATURAL BAITS

There are quite a few natural baits that all game fish feed on and they are found, naturally, in the vicinity of the specific fish that eat them. The only "stranger" in the crowd is the earthworm, which only finds its way to the stream or lake when the rain washes it in or drifts down as a wash-in into a stream that enters the lake. Yet the earthworm is the universal first choice of all freshwater fish. If you have never fished with anything else, you could enjoy a lifetime of success on all game fish, using only the earthworm.

The question then arises, why bother with anything else if this is so? The answer lies in the fact that artificial lures, in some cases and conditions, work better than worms, and some artificials work better than other artificials at certain times. This vagueness is part of the charm of angling. There is no guaranteed way of catching fish every time. No matter how much of an expert you may become, there will be days that will find you fishless, no matter how hard you try. On one evening you'll murder the trout on dry flies. The next night out, you may have to turn to the worm to bring home a fish. On another trip you'll fare well catching bass on surface plugs and bugs, but the next time in the same place under the same conditions you may catch them only with a deep-running plug or a deep-trolled live

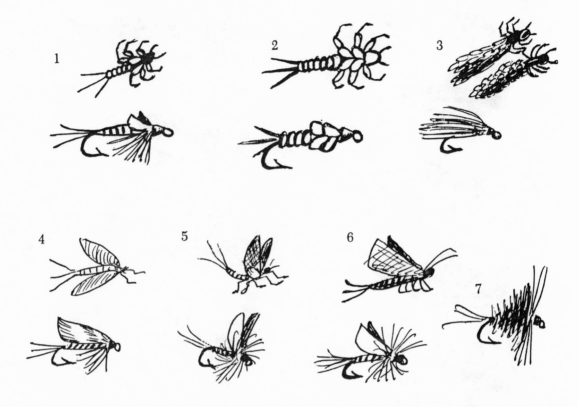

FIGURE 4-7. STREAM INSECTS AND THEIR ARTIFICIAL IMITATIONS

1] Typical mayfly nymph and, below, its nymphal imitation. 2] Stone-fly nymph and, below this, its imitation. 3] Caddis flies in cases of bark, grass and, for the second, gravel-sand. The general type of wet fly serves as the imitation. 4] Dead and floating mayfly. Below this is a typical mayfly pattern. 5] Floating and very live mayfly dun and, below it, the classical dry fly. 6] Caddis and stone flies wear their wings back, and the imitation is tied likewise. 7] Fly that seems to imitate them all—the bivisible in all colors.

bait such as a minnow or night-crawler worm. Still another time the bass may go crazy over crawfish.

So, to be well rounded and well prepared, it is best to know all of the natural baits as well as the basic forms of artificials. Being able to catch fish in different ways is a lot of fun. Just because all fish take worms is no reason to stick to this one bait for the rest of your life.

Listed and shown in Fig. 4–8 are the principal baits for all conditions of stream and lake angling.

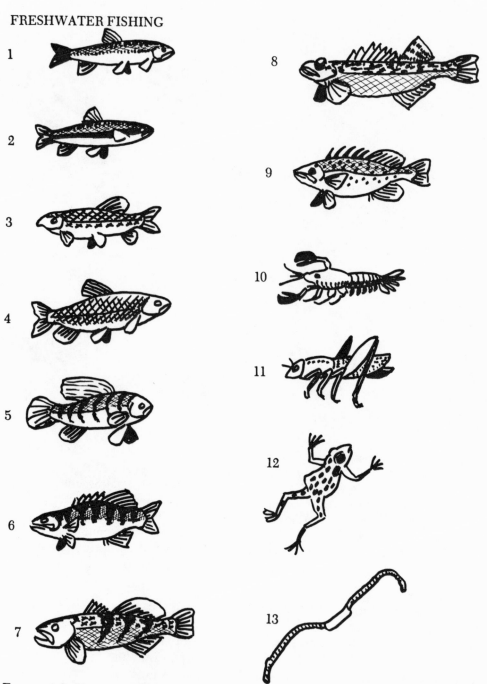

FIGURE 4-8. NATURAL BAITS

Shown on this page in enough detail for general observation and identification are the principal natural baits for all types of freshwater fishing. They are found in the natural environment of the fish to be sought.

1] Shiner minnow. 2] Blacknose dace. 3] Sucker. 4] Creek chub. 5] Killifish. 6] Small yellow perch. 7] Sculpin. 8] Darter. 9] Stickleback minnow. 10] Crawfish. 11] Grasshopper. 12] Frog. 13] Angle (earthworm).

BASIC TERMINAL RIGS

Terminal tackle is the business end of the gear setup. The variants available in this area are almost endless, but like everything else, there are the few basic requirements upon which these variants are based. I've fished all over this continent and have seen and used countless arrangements of hooks, lines, leaders, sinkers, swivels, and so forth. Today I use but a few as are shown in the following diagrams. The same goes for knots. In my Boy Scout days I knew how to tie at least twenty knots. For my fishing today I use only the bowline for tying up the boat, the blood knot for joining sections of leader or line together and the slipknot for tying on swivels, sinkers and hooks. There is no need for further complications. Learn to tie these in the dark and you are in business.

Shown and described in Figs. 4–9, 10, 11, 12, 13 are the basic terminal rigs and their uses and purposes. Study and remember them.

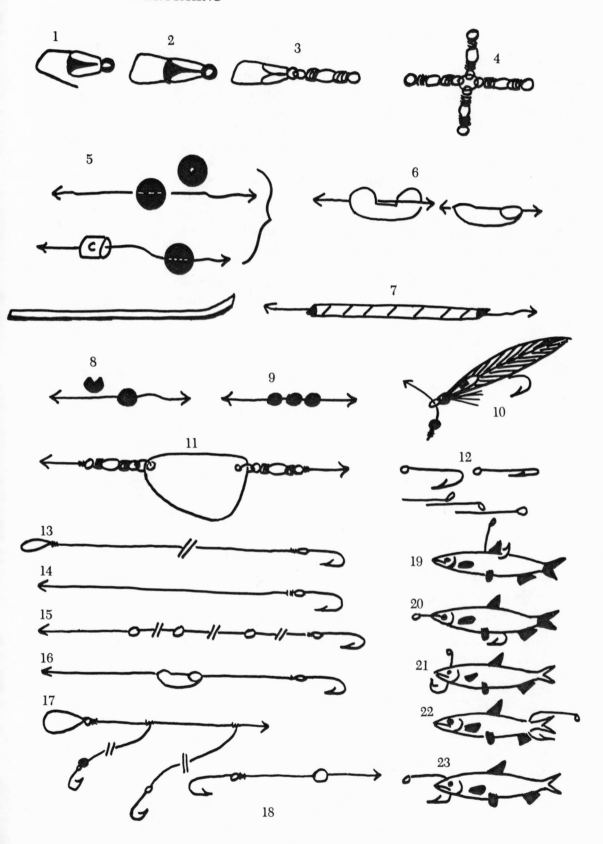

Figure 4-9. Terminal Tackle Rigs

Shown here are the various ways of assembling your terminal tackle that are necessary in all types of freshwater fishing. There are countless variations and combinations of all these "ties" and "makes," but shown here are all you need to know, at least at first. Buy all the parts and then sit down and assemble them, keeping in mind what each will be used for.

1] The snap. This is used when tied onto a leader, line or metal leader to which you snap on a lure or hook or rig. It is shown open and [*2*] closed—looks like a safety pin! *3]* The snap-swivel. This combination cuts out the twist of the lure or rig that might be caused in the casting or trolling of the terminal lure. *4]* This is the four-way swivel combination. It can be made in a three-way rig also. It is used in conjunction with tying in hooks and weights for still fishing or slow trolling. The bottom spoke can, for example, tie into the sinker. *5]* This is the heavy slip sinker with the hole in the middle. It is used as a cast weight with the line flowing through it freely. The baited hook can be taken by the fish without any noticeable drag. He can run with the bait without being scared by the weight of the lead. When he has run a bit, you can then set the hook! The drawing with the C is a cork attached well ahead of the line to help keep it off the bottom. It too has a hole big enough for the line to flow through smoothly. *6]* The clamp-on type sinker. A bit heavier than the wraparound lead or BB-shot lead. Clamps on as shown and can be more easily removed than the split-shot BB. *7]* This is the lead strip wraparound lead that can be lengthened or shortened at will for just the correct weight to solve the problem of the moment. Knots can be tied ahead and behind to keep it from slipping

on the line. *8]* The BB split shot. Merely place the line in the slot and close the lead tight. *9]* Several split shots can be clamped on at intervals. This is good for fly-rod or light-spinning casting of a weighted fly or bait. *10]* The split shot shown ahead of a streamer fly. Note that the end of the leader is knotted so that the lead will not slip off. A very effective way to weight a fly. *11]* The trolling fin. This is attached to the running line from the swivel, and the swivel behind is attached to the terminal tackle, weights and bait hooks. *12]* The offset bend hook, the straight hook, the turned-up eye hook, the turned-down eye hook and the straight eye hook. These are the basic hook eye types and their choice is really a matter of personal preference. (See hook chart, Fig. 4-12.) *13]* The leader loop and attached hook. These can be bought this way, or you can tie them in this way yourself. Also, there is a metal leader for use in bass, pike and muskie fishing which is encased in plastic for the same purpose. *14]* The hook is merely tied into a strip of leader material or directly to the line. *15]* Split shot clamped on at intervals for easy casting of the bait. *16]* The clamp-on weight shown on the leader. *17]* The plumb-shaped weight is attached to the line at the end with the two bait hooks tied in at convenient intervals up the main line. *18]* Split shot attached to the hook and leader/line. *19]* Live minnow hooked for still fishing. *20]* Live minnow hooked (now dead) through the belly with hook protruding through the belly. *21]* Hooked through the head for trolling or casting or still fishing. *22]* Hooked through the tail for light casting, still fishing. *23]* Hooked through the head with the shank forward for casting and trolling.

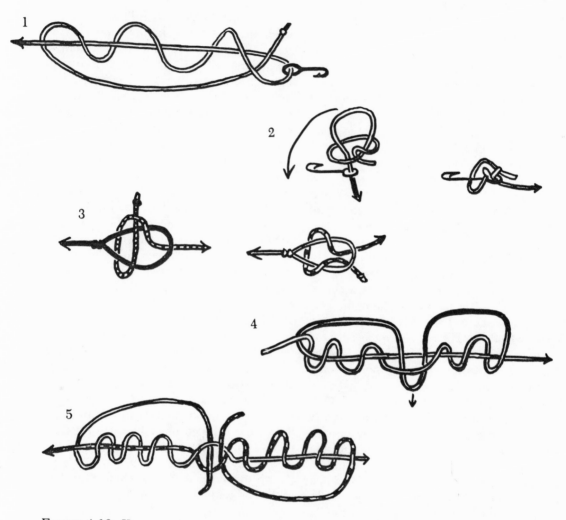

FIGURE 4-10. KNOTS

1] The simple clinch knot is surefire for quick tying on of the hook or lure to the line or leader. Put on a couple or more rolls to be sure if you like and as additional safety you can also double the end back into the wide loop at the bottom. *2]* The ancient turle knot is a good one for tying the leader onto the hook. The right diagram is a view of the completed knot. *3]* These are two variations of a simple and nonbulky way of securing the looped leader to the fly line. I prefer the second one. *4]* This is a simple way to create a loop for a looped leader.

When finished, merely pull the loop down and tighten the knot. *5]* This is the line-to-leader knot, or the best way of joining two sections of leader together, especially if you desire to leave an end long for a tippet. (The two or three dropper or tippet leader is used in two- and three-fly wet fly-fishing. Or you can use two flies of dry pattern if you prefer.)

Learn to tie these knots. Now learn to tie them in the dark. Once you can do this, you will never be at a loss to tie things up!

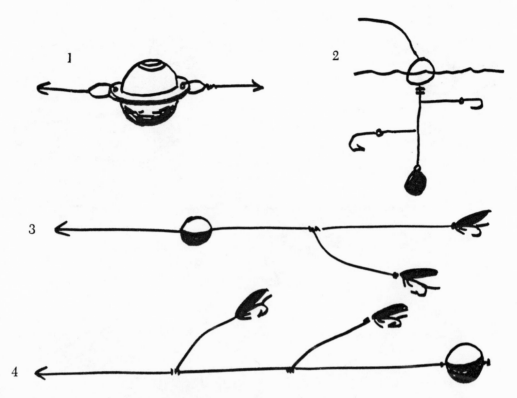

FIGURE 4-11. PLASTIC BUBBLE OR BOBBER

Shown here is the plastic bubble or "bobber" and its use in spinning. The old cork bobber has gone modern with spinning gear! Now you can cast even the daintiest of flies and small live baits to the trout by using the bobber, and still fishing, of course, is the natural use for the bobber, as it always has been. The bobber can also be used with bait-casting gear and par-ticularly with the fly rod, since it is so light. An effective use of the bobber is in conjunction with the fly rod and the closed-face spinning reel loaded with monofilament line. This can be cast great distances with ease.

1] Plastic bubble (can be weighted by adding water). *2]* Conventional "above the bait" rig. *3]* Ahead of flies. *4]* Behind flies (best for long casts).

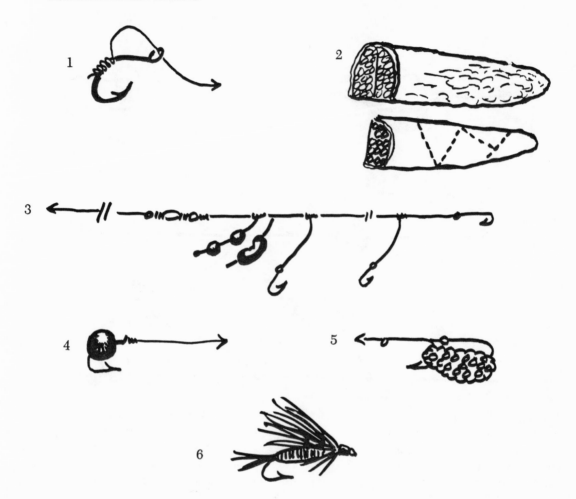

FIGURE 4-12. SPECIAL STEELHEAD RIGS

While the steelhead is a trout and can be caught by the trout-fishing methods used on all the other species, the steelhead is a bit different than the others, or at least many additional rigs are used in catching them than the conventional fly- and bait-casting techniques. Shown here are the most popular rigs.

1] Snell knot egg hookup. This is made to hold a cluster of eggs or bits of yarn that resemble salmon eggs. (Good for worms, too!) 2] Cut chunks of salmon eggs. These are hooked in various ways, such as in [1], and drifted in the current, weighted in the wintertime, during the salmon runs. The steelhead follow the salmon up the streams, feeding on the discarded eggs, and at that time they seldom take flies or lures, feeding mainly on the eggs. NOTE: Egg clusters are cut from half skein of eggs for rig [1]. 3] Weighted hook setup for drifting salmon-egg cluster. 4] Single egg on small salmon-egg hooks. 5] Cluster eggs on single hook. 6] Weighted streamer fly for use during the summer runs when the steelhead are not feeding exclusively on salmon eggs. Spinning lures, spoons and spinners also get 'em with the conventional techniques associated with trout fishing as outlined in Chapter 8.

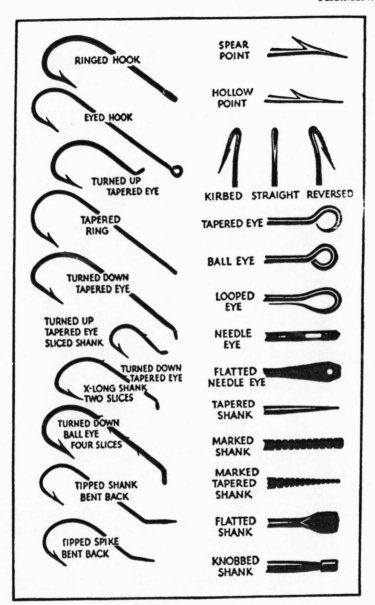

FIGURE 4-13. HOOK CHART

Shown here are the various types of hook bends, shank lengths and hook eyes used in most freshwater angling. Actually, this author has never paid too much attention to the various styles, having used all of them at one time or other. For the exact-minded researching type of tackle tinkerer, the chart is included here for your study purposes.

5 TACKLE CARE AND REPAIR

While preparing this chapter, I had the experience of shopping for a used car for a friend. When he finally decided on one, I said to him that he should now spend a hundred dollars or more on that car before he drove it, for chances are the owner didn't take care of it at all and certain parts would be worn dangerously. We looked, for example, at the front wheel bearings, and they were shot simply because they were never checked and greased. The mechanic who treated the car said that not one in a hundred car owners ever asks to check these bearings. When these bearings go, they go all of a sudden, and the front wheels can fly off. The rest of his car was in equally bad condition. The mechanic said that people blame the manufacturer for shoddy workmanship when it is their own lack of care that causes expensive repair bills. So my friend spent the hundred dollars and now he has a well-running car.

Fishing tackle demands this same kind of attention. I own a reel that my father bought fifty years ago. It is still a jewel and works perfectly because he took good care of it and so have I. I have a split bamboo rod I've owned for fifteen years, and it is as good today as it was the day I bought it.

Care of tackle is really a very simple thing. It requires a minimum amount of mechanical ability. If you can work a simple screw carefully, you can care for all your gear properly. All you need is a bit of patience and the desire to keep what you have in good order. Keep a can of good oil, some silicone, grease, a few old rags, some toothpicks and the proper tools with which to operate handy at all times and you are set.

Rust and wear are the things that tear down tackle. Contact with sand and grit cause more trouble. It is a simple matter of keeping your gear away from sand and grit, or, if you fish in a sandstorm, taking the reel apart after the trip, cleaning it and re-oiling it.

Before you put it away for the season, clean it well, re-oil and it will be all set next year. It is best to check the reels after two or three trips or any kind of hard usage and keep them oiled and cleaned.

Fly lines should be washed often, even though you use grease dressing on them, for they pick up a lot of dirt from the water. Simply run the line out on the grass and, using a dry piece of cloth, gently squeeze your way along the entire length two or three times. Then bathe the line in a very weak solution of soap and rinse it thoroughly. Let it dry and then reel the line back on the spool. The same goes for braided level lines used in spinning and bait casting.

Your rod requires constant observation, because breaks in the finish, bends in the joints or ferrules and chips or scratches in the line guides can wreck a good line in no time. Remember that the line goes through those guides with much pressure and speed. They must be dirt free and also kept free from scratches that would snag the line. If they become scratched, they should be replaced. You must learn very quickly not to let your rods bounce around in the trunk of the car or the bottom of the boat. Treat them with a bit of respect, and they will return the favor.

You have already learned how to avoid twisting the ferrules and thus scratching the sides when setting up tackle. Remember this and also remember to clean the ferrules each time before you assemble the rod to eliminate dust or grime or sand. Do not think that because the rod is made of glass that it is impervious to rot. It is not. When the surface becomes worn, clean it and then use spar varnish lightly. Put this on with the tips of your fingers and let it dry, not next to heat but in a dry place. To protect the finish of your rod, don't leave it out at night or baking all day in the sun. Wash it off after each use. On my good rods, I usually use wax a few times during the season to further protect them. It saves the messy bother of dressing down and revarnishing.

As to hooks, swivels, sinkers and the like, keep them in watertight containers. It is also a good idea to keep your lures in containers, although this is not always easy. I keep them in their boxes away from the dew, spray and bilge at the bottom of the boat.

What I am discussing here may sound too obvious to be considered, but you'd be amazed at the complete lack of respect some anglers show their gear after they have spent so much money on it. The tackle companies love those careless people!

There is really nothing complicated about caring for any of your outdoor gear, including your waders and boots, jackets and socks. Inspect them all once in a while and make the necessary replacements or repairs and you'll never be in trouble.

Don't ever throw away a rod without removing the ferrules. You never know when those spares will come in handy. Keep them in the tackle box with some wax that can be melted to set them on the rod. Keep spare parts from old reels for temporary repair and save all screws. An on-location repair may demand using them to allow you to keep on going.

A whole book could be written on tackle care, but is unnecessary if you use your common sense. Fishing tackle is really very elementary and requires only regular care to keep it running at tip-top performance.

Even if you are not a tinkerer or one who is mechanically minded, you should be able to take a reel apart and put it back together again. Practice this as a dress rehearsal for the day trouble comes.

ACCESSORIES 6

There is a host of items known as accessories. These are items of equipment other than the basic gear, terminal rigs and lures that are necessary in all types of freshwater fishing. Without them, your trip would be almost impossible. I will discuss only the most necessary, but there are all kinds of other creative gimmicks you can add to improve your fishing.

WATER TRANSPORTATION

There are times when you can fish from the shore of a pond or lake, a stream or river. When you can't, or prefer not to, some kind of water transportation is needed.

The canoe is one of the oldest forms of fishing craft. But just because America's great fishermen, the Indians, used it doesn't mean that it is the best kind. A canoe is tippy and hard to handle in a wind. It is beautiful to use when on a small lake or pond out of the wind, or when you can pick your times to fish and be sure the water is smooth and the wind is down. Paddling or drifting along, you can approach a good fishing spot with hardly a ripple and not disclose your presence to the fish. Learn not to bounce tackle and tackle boxes around in the bottom of the canoe for these vibrations will carry over into the fish's ears (the lateral line of sense organs shown on p. 116). The same applies to tackle banging and paddle or oar rattling in all other kinds of craft.

The small rowboat, with or without a motor, is the most practical water transportation, for you can stand up in it to cast.

But you must be careful, particularly if two of you are fishing together. If you are going any distance or intend to do a lot of trolling with the small rowboat, a small outboard is a blessing, though again, try and use it to the minimum, approaching your fishing spot (for casting or still fishing) with the motor turned off. It is best to row to the spot so as not to scare the fish. Larger pleasure-type outboards with bigger motors are also recommended, but you should have higher sides if you are fishing a big lake or broad river, since the wind can whip up quite a bit of dangerous waves. Use judgment in your ventures and do not go out in rough weather. The fish can wait and so can you. Also, be sure to leave the scene if a storm is seen approaching or if rain is obviously going to fall.

FOOTGEAR

If you are going to fish from the shore of the lake, you'll need footgear designed to keep your feet warm and dry. Hip boots are the most practical for this, since they can be rolled down if you are not wading out into deep water. When you wish to wade, you can pull them up and attach them by the strap to your belt. Wear a pair of wool socks and fold your pant legs smoothly and comfortably so that there is little friction on your legs.

Hip boots can also be used for stream wading, although hip-deep wading is usually required, and the added protection of hip or chest waders is advised. Good chest waders are quite expensive, so try and use the boots as much as possible. The chest waders are usually only used when the angler is fly-fishing or spinning a big river or wishes to wade well out from the shore of a lake. In buying chest waders, or even hip waders, make sure you choose a loose fit, since a tight one will restrict leg motion greatly, and undue strain on the seams will cause them to part even before the first season has ended.

Waders come in two styles: the boot foot, which is the same as the rubber boot with the boot attached to the cloth top section, and the stocking foot, which requires wearing a pair of socks over the wader and then the addition of a pair of wading shoes. The former is preferred and is simpler. Both boot bottoms have additional aids in wading for different types of ground. The ordinary cutout boot bottoms suffice for most wading, but if you are wading in slimy streams and clean slick rocks, a pair of felt attachments is recommended. If wading mostly in gravel, rocks and sand, a set of chains can be slipped on over the boot foot.

JACKETS

Fishing or wading jackets come in two basic lengths—long and short. The long are quite sufficient for most cold weather or windy use when fishing from the boat or wading in shallow water. However, if you plan to wade in chest waders, a jacket of short length is advised, since the bottom of the long jacket would be constantly in the water, wetting the food and gear you keep in your pockets. Both jacket types have generous pockets for carrying lure boxes and accessories such as food, cigarettes or even a plastic raincoat. You should wear a hat, since you'll be out in the hot sunshine or in the cold wind. The visor type is recommended, because you'll have your eyes on the water and will need the shade. Polaroid glasses are an excellent addition, either in prescription if you already wear glasses, or just plain, if you do not. Slip-on lenses are most impractical.

TACKLE BOX AND LURE CONTAINERS

You should really have three of these: one for the home stockpile, a second and large one for the boat and then a third for the car. Your basic stock should be large unless you like to make constant trips to the tackle store. Also, you may decide to fish at night after closing time at the store and must have what you need at hand. It is a good idea to buy a large supply of equipment, particularly lures, at the beginning of the season, so that you will never be without them.

As I have indicated before, the terminal-tackle parts should be kept apart in separate watertight compartments or containers (plastic for carrying, or glass if kept in the tackle box). Flies are filed neatly in special fly boxes. Dry flies are kept in boxes that are sectionalized so as not to crush the delicate fibers, and wet-fly boxes are used for the wets, nymphs and streamers. Spinning lures should be kept in a box with slot sections or, preferably, in their own containers so that there is no danger of hooks snagging or tangling.

Much of what is described here is easier seen at the tackle store. Present your case to the tackle salesman for his advice and also keep an eye on other anglers and see how they arrange their gear.

Tools such as small pinch pliers, various size screwdrivers and additional screws and parts are good to have along in case of a streamside repair or a reel repair out on the lake. A small container of oil is helpful for additional lubrication. Small bits of rags are also a necessity for quick cleaning needs.

STAFF AND NETS

If you are new at wading the fast stream, a wading staff that can be the ringless discard from the ski outfit is perfect, as it has a strap handle. A simple one can be made from an old broom handle that is not rotted. Simply attach a leather strap to the top end and have the other end shaved to a point. When not in use, it can be attached to your belt.

For stream fishing a short-handled net, similar in size to a tennis racket, is required and is attached to a stretch cord which, in turn, is snapped to the wading jacket. This is for use in landing the fish when you are in the water.

A boat net is the same general shape as the wading net, but with a longer handle, usually about two to three feet in length. Both nets come in wood or metal, with either firm or collapsible hoops. (I prefer the former, since they are always instantly available and in working order.)

FISH KEEPERS AND BAIT BOXES

In order to keep your bait fish alive, a bait can is advised for boat fishing. It can be tied to a rope and be lowered over the side for fresh water. Remember to bring it in when you start the motor to move to another spot or go home!

Live bait that is carried by the stream angler is carried in a very small bait can and is dipped into the water frequently so that the bait fish will not suffocate.

To keep your fish *catch* when fishing from a boat, a fish stringer which contains a succession of very large safety-pin-type rigs is recommended. The fish is attached by hooking the pin part through the lower jaw so that the fish can breathe freely in the water when the boat is stopped. In this way it is almost as if he is free. Also, remember to haul in the stringer when you are about to take off and then keep the fish in the shade. If you have a cold box aboard, it is better to kill the fish, clean them and place the sections in the box.

The old-style bamboo fishing *creel* is worn by the stream angler to store his trout or bass, but many of the newer types of fishing jackets have air-vented creels on the back of the jacket with removable rubber linings so that the creel can be easily and frequently washed.

Insects are fish food, but also will use *you* for a meal. So take along insect repellent (*6-12* is the best I've found) and keep it in your tackle box or pocket away from the lures and leaders.

A medicine kit is necessary, complete with a needle that has been sterilized and wrapped, Band-Aids and bandage material, cotton and medicine, including sunburn oil and aspirin. A small bottle of drinking water aboard the boat is also recommended. Juicy food in the form of apples and oranges is also good insurance against thirst.

And finally, bring your fishing license. Make sure this is in your wallet, or if you are the ultracareful type, leave your wallet in your car and carry the license in a waterproof container in your pocket. A copy of the fish laws is also good to have along just in case you have a problem remembering the fish length and fish number for your day's outing.

Now we are ready to go fishing.

7 A PANFISHING EXCURSION

On your first trip out, panfish will be the goal, and a lot of fun they'll be. They are not big fish, and they do not strain your tackle. But they'll help you familiarize yourself with your tackle and with the actual fun of fishing.

We'll go armed with the tackle you have bought and learned to setup and cast. We'll also have my tackle box and gear to draw on if necessary.

The panfish number quite a few species. We have the big sunfish family of which there are about three varieties in almost every lake. Then there is the bluegill, the crappie, the yellow and the white perch. We have our fly rods set up and our light spinning gear. We've a can of worms and a box of small lures and basic terminal tackle.

As we walk down toward the dock, we see a broken shoreline around the lake graced with huge boulders, stretches of sandy beach and shoreline patches where the foliage dips into the water. Alders, birches, maples and a few evergreens such as pine, spruce and a hemlock show up dark against the paler greens of the leaf trees. A hawk circles lazily over a horizon laden with a few puffy clouds. The day is warm, and summer insects are buzzing in the bushes.

Right near the dock where our little rowboat is tied up there is a small grouping of pond lilies and grass. An old sunken tree lies out there half submerged. There are two turtles sunning themselves on one of the branches.

Even before we think of the boat, our fishing starts right at the dock. As we walk softly on the dock planks, we look overboard down at the bottom. Sunnies. A whole group of them. We are going to learn a good lesson here.

Are you all rigged up?

Fine.

Now impale an earthworm on your size-12 hook (no sinker needed) and, using the fly rod, dangle that worm over the side, letting it sink down among the sunfish.

See. Here they come. Several of them.

One bites at the worm. You pull it up. Ah, you're too quick. Put it down again.

There they come, teasing the bait this time.

There. One has taken the worm into his mouth, but he spit it out again. See, it isn't as easy as you thought. But this is how they act when they are not hungry. Right at the start, the surefire lure, the earthworm, which you thought would catch you a mess of fish, has proven to be a potential failure.

But look out, here comes a bigger fish. It's a yellow perch. He's coming in fast. There, he's grabbed the bait. Now, PULL UP!

Your first fish!

In comparison with what you'll be catching later, he's a relatively small one, so put him back, gently. Grasp him lightly behind the gill fin and unhook him. Then set him in the water so that he will swim away from you. Don't just throw him back.

You'll follow that procedure as you fish through this chapter, and it is hoped, through all your fishing days. Put them back for another day and another angler!

Now for those lily pads and that old sunken tree. What do you say we try some dry flies and float them right in there next to the pads. All set? OK. Make your cast, but be careful. There's little back-cast room here on the dock, and I don't wish to get a fly stuck in my face. So roll cast is the ticket. Use a big, fluffy, dry fly, saturate it with the fly dope that's in your tackle to make the flies float. Blow off the excess and wipe your fingers before you touch your leader, or else it will float to, which you don't want it to do. Now tie the fly onto the leader tippet.

Roll out the cast. Ah, that's it. Let the fly float there a few seconds. Oops. There's your first surface hit. He missed. Leave the fly there.

There he is again. Missed. Now see how quick you are. Next time he hits, anticipate a bit and strike with a little pressure . . . just enough to barb the fish.

Hit. Strike! That's it. He's on!

Look at him jump and thrash. Gradually retrieve the line, keeping a generous amount of pressure on the rod and keeping that rod up like you will when you encounter much bigger adversaries, such as a big brown trout or a rainbow in a fast stream. Play him out and then bring him in to your net. Submerge the net almost to the handle. Now lead the fish into the net. Careful. He doesn't want to give up yet and he let's you know with an explosive blast for freedom at the sight of the net. Once again now, lead him in. This time he's had it for sure. Scoop him up, relax the rod.

Pretty little pumpkinseed? Pretty as the prettiest trout.

Now let's try spinning. We'll tie a Colorado spinner of small size on the three-pound test line of your ultralight spinning gear. That will be easy to cast, and you'll have quite a time with whatever takes it. To add to the attractiveness, put a worm on two of the hooks. Cast it gently now, so as not to flip the worm off. Hook it on this way.

Make your cast beyond the old tree into that spot that looks deeper. As soon as the lure hits the water, start your retrieve by cranking the reel handle and closing the pickup bale which will bring in the line.

Note the sparkle of the spinner blade. There's a fish behind it already. Keep reeling in slowly.

Bang! A hit and he's on.

Put your rod up now and, with your reel hand, keep pressure against the fish. Look at your rod bend! He's on a rush, and your reel's sensitive *brake* or drag lets some line go. Boy, what a ruckus he's causing out there. It's a good-size crappie and he's scrappy! Play him, brother, and you are now a member of the angling fraternity. He'll make a nice photograph if you land him.

Now let's get into our rowboat and take a look at our lake. I'll row. You sit in the stern seat. Place your tackle box at your feet in the center of the bottom, and I'll place mine up ahead of my seat.

We'll row out a bit from shore and scan the lake for a good spot to fish. Over on that far shore there are some big rocks along the edge, and I see several rock tops protruding through the surface. That's a good spot to head for. But on the way we'll troll and cast just to see what we can pick up in the way of action.

We'll troll a spinning rod, the medium-size rig, so we can use the ultralight for casting. On that troll, let's rig up an Indiana spinner and a worm. Use the ultralight with a small, diving, zigzagging plug. We'll set up the fly rod with a couple of wet flies, just for variety. Quite a setup for our panfish.

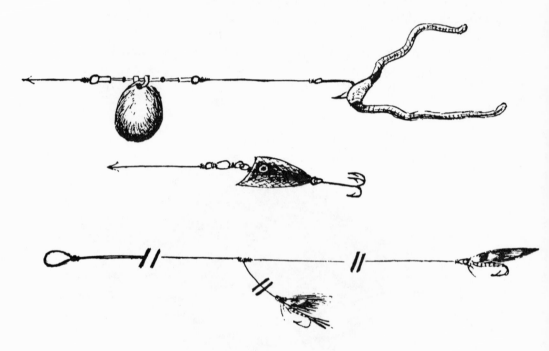

Drop your troll overboard, with the drag set well under the line breaking strength. I'll row hard for a few strokes just to get the boat moving. The water is fairly deep here and, despite its clarity, I can't see the bottom, so there is no chance of snagging.

For the time being, you can cast the plug out to the other side of the boat and just let it troll in parallel to the bait. It will stay near the surface so they will not tangle. We'll hold the fly rod until we reach our destination.

If we were to troll deeper, we would add a weight to the line as shown in Chapter 4 on terminal tackle. Perhaps later, we'll do a bit of still-fishing right in the spot we are trolling over right now. They tell me at the local tackle store that there are a lot of good catfish in the deeper parts of the lake, and this seems to be one of them. Watch that bait rod. Better hold it so you can feel the hit if a fish strikes. I'll row slowly now so that the rig will sink farther down. The plug will barely wobble, which makes it quite irresistible. Wonder which one the fish will take? You're betting on the worm?

You're right. Wow! That's a good strike. Raise the rod. It's bending and vibrating, so you know that you've a good fish. Keep the rod tension strong by reeling in the line against it. I'll bring in the plug so you won't tangle with it. Now your fish is up on the surface. He's a jumper. That's a white perch, and since they swim in schools there will be others around. Bring him in now. That's it. Cast the unbaited spinner out there again, let it sink down a few feet and begin the retrieve. There. Another strike. You keep fishing on that side and I'll try to attract one on the little plug on this side.

After three casts and no luck, I change to a tiny spinning spoon of silver color and immediately get a strike and another white perch to tail you—one to three!

Now, just for variety, remembering that white perch feed on little minnows, pick up the fly rod. I've taken off the dry-fly leader and replaced it with a dropper leader and two tinsel-bodied wet-bucktail-type flies, just the ticket for white perch. Stand up now and cast on an angle behind the boat. The angle is so that you will not catch me on the backswing.

There you go. A strike on the first cast just as the fly hit the water. See the water breaking up in several places. The school of fish is right on the surface now, and that's good! Bring him in and cast again. There you've got *two* fish on this time. How about that!

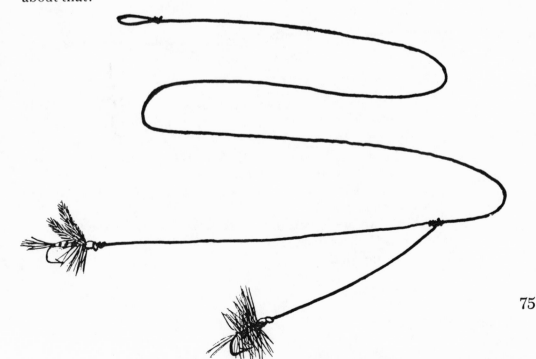

We could stay out here all day and catch a pailful of perch, but I want you to get the taste of some bluegill fishing over there in the shallows and in much of that cove. On the outer edge are the lily pads and grass, but a narrow channel winds through them to to the mucky and weedy shoreline. That's where you'll find the bluegills—sitting under the shade of the alders.

Use the ultralight spinning gear and a small wiggling, popping plug. Cast it in there. You may get snagged, but make the cast anyway. You may get hung up on the retrieve, but the actual moment of the cast is the important thing here. That's usually when the fish will take the lure. Bluegills are of the sunfish family and, despite their small size, they are heavily built and are full of fight. You'll see in a moment.

There goes your cast. Let the lure sit for an instant and float there enticingly. Now retrieve the line slowly and carefully and merely move the lure without bringing it forward. Bang! See what I mean? He's on. Look at your little rod bend and listen to the music of that drag releasing line. Careful, he's going to hang you up in the brush and tangle. He knows just where to head for.

A beautiful dark-colored fish. The *blue* of the bluegill is the gunmetal hue of the coloration and the bright iridescent blue peg at the corner of the gill.

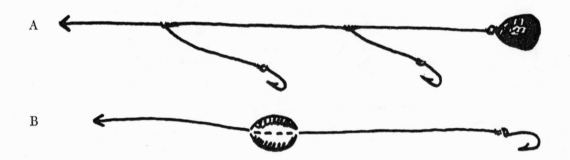

He'll taste good in the evening meal.

Now let's try for some catfish out in the middle of the lake.

That calls for still-fishing and a special terminal-tackle rig. Two rigs for variety. The first will be the two-hook rig with the weight at the bottom. You'll use that one while I try the slip-sinker combination and cast it a distance away. We'll see which one attracts a cat.

Since we are armed only with worms, they'll have to do for the cat. He likes them. He also likes all kinds of meat and smelly baits of any kind.

OK, let's see who gets the first strike. Remember that the catfish does not strike hard. You'll first feel a slight nibble on your line causing some tension and telegraphing the need for action. My rig will not show this, but I'll know that one is on and has taken the bait firmly when the line begins to travel out through the guides. In my case, I leave the bail open and the line absolutely free to run.

Your cast is out. So is mine. We'll just sit here and wait. Panfishing fun? You bet it is. After years of fishing in all corners of the globe for the biggest of the game fish you'll return to this pond or some small lake where you live and you'll delight, as you have today, in a basic style of fishing that proves that it doesn't really matter what fish you are angling for, just so long as you are angling. You're out in the open, away from city life, tensions and the confusions of progress and civilization. You're away from it all and you can relax.

Hey, your dreaming caught you off guard. You didn't see that rod tip bounce. Pick up your rod now and feel for the next exertion of pressure from the cat. Feel it? He's on. Pull up a bit and see what happens. Merely raise your rod tip in pressure against the line. If the rod tip flutters a bit, he's on. But don't just reel in slowly. Jab him. Give the hook a good solid yank. There. Uh oh, he's off. Better reel in and inspect your bait. He took it! Rig up another worm and lower the outfit again.

There's action on my line. See it pay out from the reel, ever so slowly. I wonder if the cat really has the bait in his mouth, or if he is just fooling with it like those sunnies did back at the dock. Well, we'll just let him run a bit and then we'll snub him.

That seems to be a long enough run. Look at that rod tip bounce. He's on. He doesn't fight hard. Messy to remove from the hook because of the spikes. We'll just cut the leader above the hook and put him into the water pail with the others. We'll save the hook when we clean him.

Since you have witnessed several kinds of panfishing, let's try dry flies. We'll row over to the edge of the lily pads right in front of the dock, and you can dry fly-fish to your heart's content. Glad you chose this method, since it is the sportiest of them all for both little fish and big trout. You can stand up and cast from the boat.

This experience will give you the opportunity to try out your fore-and-aft cast, the curve cast, the roll pickup and the roll cast. Use your light fly rod, the double-tapered line and the nine-foot leader tapered to 3X. On the tippet end we'll tie in a foot and a half of 4X leader for extra thinness for use with very small flies. Want to use wets or drys?

Drys? Fine. You see the real action better that way.

Remember these sequences; they'll pay off when you hit the trout stream.

Well, so far today we've still-fished for sunnies at the dock, fly-fished for the sunfish, spin-fished lures for the white perch and small bucktails. Not a bad start.

Now we'll have a nice meal.

GOING AFTER LARGER FISH 8

PICKEREL

Next we will take one step up on the angling ladder, and catch
a chain pickerel. This experience will stand you in good favor
when the time comes for you to catch his big brothers, the pike
and the muskie. It is basically the same experience but with ten
times the fight. There's also a chance that we may hang into a
largemouth bass. Both species are usually found in the same lake
and often in the same locations.

We're on another lake this time. Possibly a lake in Connecticut, among the tree-covered hills on a sultry August day
with the sun beating down on us. It could be in a more northern
lake, say in Maine, with that same sun burning down, but the
air tempered with less humidity and a slight coolness in the
breeze. Or we could be fishing a Florida lake where the biggest
bass hang out and the locals don't look twice, unless the pickerel
goes over five pounds or the bass over twelve pounds! Pickerel
abound in all the Midwest lakes too and in the far West.

If we troll, we could hit a pickerel or a bass. If, however, we
try for a pickerel in a thick weed bed where they are known to
feed and hang out, we are pretty sure of our adversary.

From this moment on, you are in for a lot of lure and rig hang-
ups. I was easy with you in panfishing, for we fished in areas
where there were few weeds and enough space between the pads
so that you were lucky enough not to get hung up. Now I'll take
you right into a veritable forest of grasses, weeds, old tree snags
and whatnot. You'll cast in there or troll through it and

frequently get hung up. You'll learn that this is part of the game. We'll show you some so-called weedless lures, but you'll still get your measure of stalls where you'll have to reel in. We may even have to push the boat into the snag to rescue your lure or plug.

The pickerel is primarily a bait feeder, preferring minnows and small fish of its own species. He is a voracious fellow, feeding, like his bass friends, on anything that moves. He's not as dramatic as the bass and usually follows a lure for some distance before he decides to take it. This is not a definite rule though. Pickerel will sometimes hit a lure or fly the instant it hits the water, so watch out.

First we'll cast right along the edge of a shallow section of the lake. It is crowded on the outside with grass stems that extend just above the water. Behind them are some pads. Beyond this you can see arrowroot, pads, lakeweed and finally, close to the shore, fallen trees and muck. This is a channel leading from a tiny brook that enters the lake back there in the brush. It is a great place for good-sized pickerel, though they are found in many other parts of the lake as well.

You'll start casting with the big fly rod, the one you will later use for bug fishing for bass. Your lure is one of my creations, a *weedless* feather fly in the shape of a bucktail. We've guarded

the hook as best we can and feathered the fly thickly to help guard that hook from snagging. You can cast it with some confidence into the snags, but we'll test your accuracy by aiming a few feet into the grass where you are not likely to get hung up. This will give you the opportunity to test out your casting skill with the big rod and the heavy line. The fly is not very light, so, to begin with, do not cast more than forty feet.

This is what your fly looks like, and you can tie it on the end of the leader.

We'll also be using the weedless plug shown in the diagram when we take up the spinning rod.

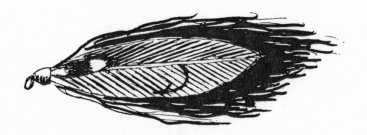

Strip out the line, about twenty feet of it, by wobbling it out with the rod tip, roll-pickup and start your false cast with the heavy fly. Careful with your angle now so that you don't catch either of us with it. You'll have to maintain height with this fly so that it won't hit the water, particularly on the back cast.

Go ahead and begin to cast, gradually lengthening your throws. Put the fly right into the outside stretch of the grass, let it set for an instant and then begin the retrieve by jerking the rod tip and pulling on the line. You'll master this action with a little practice.

Those are good first casts, but now get a little bolder! Go in there and risk a snag. Let the fly land and, with your rod held as high as possible, flip the fly over the grasses. When it comes to an open spot, let it sink just a bit. Snap! There's your first strike. It's a pickerel, all right. If it were a bass, all hell would be breaking loose. A pickerel will often stand still when hooked in the weeds, trying to decide what to do next. But the bass doesn't think. He simply explodes.

Pressure the fish. Now you've started him, and he will begin to tear up the weed patch. Pull hard on him now, using your line hand to apply backward pressure to the vertical rod. Pull him out. Bends your rod doesn't he? He doesn't want to come out, but keep the pressure to him. Look at him body-roll.

Get him out in the open. That's it. Now you have the battle on your own terms. He comes in quickly and easily, but look out now. You are in for the surprise. He's close to the boat, sees it and suddenly he's in the air again. This time to get a look at you. Hold that line tight and bend that rod into him. Keep up the pressure and let him body-roll. Pretty little pickerel, probably about two pounds.

Now I'll net him for you. Bring him in close. Easy now in case he explodes again. Easy. Ah, that's it, he swam right into the net. It is easier to unhook fish if you let them slip back into the net, since the hooks will be on top. Now you have your first pickerel.

Let's give the spinning gear a trial. We'll head for a reef of rocks where there is underwater lakeweed. There are bass there, too, though in this lake they do not grow too big. We'll troll by the spot using a spoon and a jointed plug just to see what we can stir up. If we get no action we'll go in there and cast along the drop-off.

Our trolling pattern will look like the diagram below as we traverse the shore. At various points we can reel in and do a bit of casting before we reach the reef of rocks.

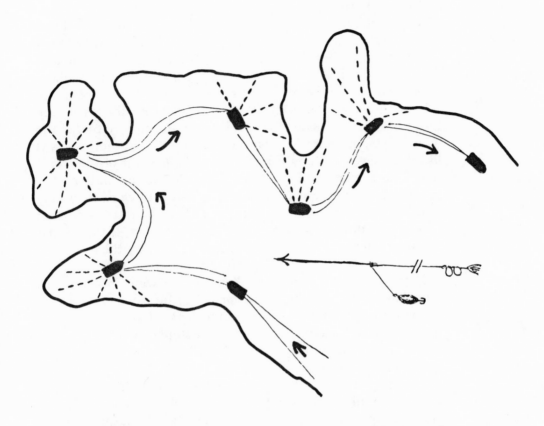

Our deep-troll rig is made up of a spoon for a weight and spinners and fly combination on the end. This is a good rig for deep trolling for bass, pike, muskie and trout.

Just for the practice, we'll use the bait-casting rod and reel for this. Set up the rig on the end of the braided line and drop it overboard as I start the motor into a slow troll. Set the drag so that it can take a lot of strain before it lets go. Prop the rod up against the seat, or better still, hold it to get the feel of this type of troll. I'll rig the spinning rod with a jointed minnow plug that floats in case we have to stop to unweed you or to fight a fish.

Just one important point to remember about that bait-casting reel: If a fish hits, you have no antireverse as you do with the spinning reel. This means, that if you snag, and the line pulls out quickly, the reel handle will spin. Watch your knuckles. You'll learn to palm the spinning handle until you can easily stop it and then tighten up, allowing the drag to let out the line.

We're in business.

As you progress in lake fishing, you'll find that most of the time you are fish-hunting instead of fishing. Unless you know a lake well, you'll use up a lot of time trolling the shoreline and working the center-of-the-lake deep spots and inviting shallow weed beds. You'll discover that there will be little action on the side of the lake where the wind is headed and the waves are breaking. On that side, the fish become uncomfortable. If the wind is lying in that direction for a few days, that shoreline will likely be devoid of any fish. So work the *lee* (out-of-the-wind) side. This is a rule to follow in all lake fishing, no matter what species of fish you are after. It is also better to work the shady side in the morning and evening rather than the side that receives the direct rays of the rising or setting sun. If the wind is coming straight down the lake, you'll have to try the coves and areas where the wind is less forceful and the water is calm.

Hey, your rod tip jumped. You weren't watching. But you must have felt it. Maybe only a snag? Not this time. That's a hit from something! Look at that handle spin. Grab the rig, and palm in on the handle. Now that you've stopped it, the fish is still taking line as the drag is letting it go. It takes quite a fish to do that. Probably a bass.

He stopped. Either he's off or he's a pickerel. Tighten up on him. Don't allow him any slack line, or he'll throw a fit. Up with that rod tip and start reeling in, but be ready for a sudden lunge or sudden stop. That's it. Fine.

Fight him, man. Keep reeling him in and gauge your reeling by that tension curve on the rod. Keep it coming. Pulls, doesn't he?

There now, he's on the surface. Quite a scrapper.

Pickerel all right. He's coming in easy, as they always do, but watch out.

Close to the boat now. I've got my rig in so you won't get tangled in it. When fishing with a partner always make it a rule that the line that is not active be pulled in immediately to get it out of the way.

Look at him swim by. That's a real keeper, a big one for this lake. He'll go three pounds. Careful now, he'll explode. Keep that rod up. Look at him take your line. Out he goes again to fight down deep now. Keep him from reaching the bottom and fouling you up in the weeds. That's another one of their tricks. Ah, you saved him, and he's up again on the surface. Bring him in slowly, and I'll net him for you. Try to let him drift back into the net this time. That's it. He's in the boat. Watch that other lure now. Flip it into the boat.

Now let's head for the rocks and do a bit of casting.

Take the spinning rod and the jointed plug and fire away. I'll guide the boat slowly down the reef and, for practice sake, you can try to see just how close to the rocks you can cast. Might as well learn it here, for in most bass fishing it is important to be able to put that lure right to the very edge of the snags, rocks, weed beds and into the pockets among the grass. The practice here will give you good control of your tackle, and soon we'll put you into some good largemouth-bass water and hope that you'll boat a few nice ones.

Pickerel fishing is a lot of fun. Most of the time, however, you'll find yourself hooking pickerel when you are bass fishing. You will seldom make a trip specifically to catch pickerel. You'll find them in the darndest places, most often where you'll not expect to find them. As you learn the technique that you'll use on bass, you will pick up a lot of pickerel for your score.

Quite often you'll hook pickerel when still-fishing with live bait for bass.

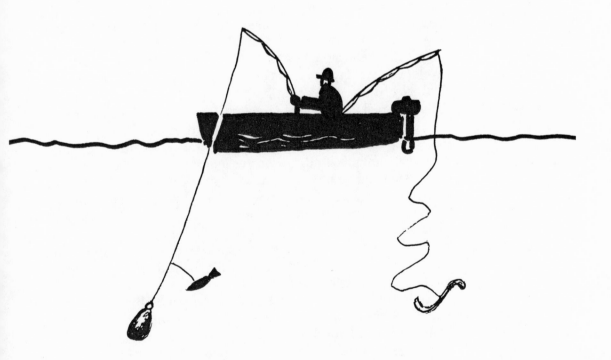

BASS

Unlike trout fishing, which started in Europe, American bass fishing began in the grass-roots experience of the pioneer days. At that time the bass was considered strictly a food fish. It was netted, caught on handlines, or taken by long poles and cord or horsehair lines tied to crude hooks, sinkers and live bait. Any athletic pleasure gained by these methods was secondary.

Later into the eighteenth century, as more men and even a few women began to fish for the fun of it, the bass gained in popularity as a game fish. Anglers were limited to horsehair lines, long heavy "poles" and single-action reels imported from Europe. There were no lures widely available other than big wet-style salmon flies. What little tackle that was obtainable was quite costly.

But sport-loving Americans, and those who wanted to catch food in more efficient ways, were quick to develop tackle to fit the nature of this popular, powerful fish. In 1810 George Snyder of Paris, Kentucky, developed a fishing reel with a multiplying gear which permitted four turns of the spool to one of the handle. This basic principle is still used in the modern bait-casting reel along with such refinements as the level-wind mechanism and controlled drag that have come from modern designers. The new reel not only enabled the angler to cast heavy baits, but also to retrieve the line faster and offer more pressure against the fighting action of the bass. Later the Meek reel was developed, an improved version made and popularized by the Kentucky firm of Meek & Milan.

But the reel alone was not enough. The rods of the day were as long as eighteen feet and rather awkward to use. To correct this situation, Dr. James Henshall, the Izaak Walton of early America, designed rods of shorter lengths which could cast the heavy natural baits and sinkers in coordination with the multiplying reel. He also wrote the first American book on bass fishing, which has become an often quoted classic. The doctor's ideas were refined when Samuel Philippe, a Pennsylvania gunsmith, introduced the use of split sections of bamboo and shorter tapered rods in order to bring the rod, reel and casting weight into better harmony.

Up to this time bass were fished for only with live bait. Either a glob of worms or an impaled minnow weighted properly with a sinker and a bobber to keep the rig off the bottom and away from the underwater snags were used. The first artificial bass lure was devised by Julio Buel, who cut a spoon from its handle and, after drilling holes in each end, attached a hook to it. He promptly took bass after bass, and soon fishermen were frantically converting the discarded family spoons into bass lures. With certain modifications this lure remains one of the best.

The search for better bass lures continued, however. One was invented by James Heddon when he whittled a length of old broom handle into the shape of a minnow and attached hooks to it. It cast well and looked like a wounded minnow to the bass. Since then, wooden plugs and, more recently, plugs made of metal or plastic have grown very popular. At first, the plugs had to be large to balance the cumbersome tackle, but through the years, with the development of lighter tackle, they have been designed smaller and smaller, down to the size of the fly-rod and ultralight spinning plugs we see today.

In the early 1940s spinning tackle arrived in this country and began a new era in American bass fishing.

Today there are many more lakes and rivers that contain bass than there were when America was first settled. Waters have been stocked with both species, and the bass have thrived where trout have disappeared due either to too much fishing activity or pollution. Roads have made access to prime bass waters open to the public. Extensive conservation practices in the national parks and forests and the commercial tree farms have helped to develop fine bass-fishing waters. Lakes that are fished hardest usually produce the larger fish, for too many bass in a given water tend to stunt the population.

Largemouth Bass

A whole book could be written on fishing for bass. So to put the art of bass fishing between the few pages allotted here is difficult. But I'll take you fishing and teach you some of the tricks of catching America's favorite fish.

First, some principles. The black bass is a voracious fish. He'll strike at almost any kind of lure when he's hungry. Find him in the shallows when he has left the deep part of the lake to go there for food, throw shallow-running, surface-popping and zigzagging plugs at him, and you've got him. Even if he's stationed permanently in a pocket in a shallow, weeded area, you'll get results since he's always on the alert to guard his lair and to hit anything that moves. If he's stationed in a midlake pad patch or grass bed, you'll find him hiding in the holes, just waiting for a minnow or your plug to whip by. Fish for him in

the deep by either trolling or by still-fishing with weighted live bait or, better still, unweighted baits. Troll for him across the deepest parts of the lake in the hot summer months or over the spring holes in the lake where he's standing out the hot temperatures from above. You'll take him. Troll the sandy shore. Troll in and out of the coves, pausing to cast into all the nooks and crannies between the weed patches. Troll the mouths of rivers and creeks, for you'll find him there. And you'll catch him.

And yet, you can also fish in all these places and many times come home without so much as a strike! That is the mystery of bass fishing.

I have performed all the new tricks that have become popular during the last fifteen or twenty years, and more often than not, I have come home fishless, or at least without a bass worth taking home. At other times, I have been with first timers who have known nothing about what they were doing and have come home with a limit of fish in a half hour. That's bass fishing.

Experience argues that night fishing for bass can be the most exciting but also the most exasperating sport yet devised by man. The times I've taken big bass at night, I've hooked bigger ones than during any daytime. And yet I've no record book big enough to list the nights that I've returned fishless. I've fished for bass more times and harder than most anglers in this country and I think I know just about all there is to know about how to catch them. An expert, you know, is a man with whom you go fishing and, if nobody catches anything, knows all the reasons why!

The largemouth bass is not a wizard. He is only a fish lacking Madison Avenue savvy and with no amount of gray matter. He's not fooling the fishermen and could care less about it. He's merely doing what comes naturally. To find the most efficient ways to net him requires a quick eye, sixth and seventh senses and a lot of luck.

My choice of method to catch old blackey is using the big fly rod and the bass bug. Perhaps it is because of my early years of orientation in fly-fishing for trout, but to me bass bugging is the grandest way to catch bass. It requires the best of balanced tackle, a strong arm, lots of patience, a host of well-tied bass bugs and some eager fish to take them.

There are millions of bass out there in the lakes and rivers and they are just waiting for you. Learn the tricks of bass bugging and you'll enjoy the highest angling thrills and partake in the finest art of fishing that has yet been devised.

Your casting will have to be well nigh perfect, avoiding snags, and placing that bug right where it ought to be—right in there between the lily pads, inside a ridge of rocks and gravel, beside an old stump or underwater log or by a big old boulder. Place it so that the bug actually bounces off into the water. If there is a bass in there, that bug'll be irresistible to him. Boy, what a pounce he'll make on that lure. He'll terrify you.

Practice your casting during the day, and fish for bass with the bug at night. Fish either from a boat drifted quietly about sixty feet from shore, or you can traverse the shoreline, without having to push your way through brush and tangles, especially during the hot summer months when it is down and clear.

The accessible lakes that are fished hard produce the best bass. Lakes where little fishing pressure is found usually find the bass smaller due to overbreeding. But, these bass are not easy to catch. Chances are they've been hooked before and have seen types of lure. The lakes around New York City contain some of the best bass fishing I have ever experienced, yet the bass there are really hard to come by. By contrast, the bigmouths of the Florida lakes and rivers, such as the St. Johns, are bigger, and there are many more real whoppers there. They are much easier to catch, or so it seems, if due to the tremendous number of them. Lakes in Georgia, Alabama, Mississippi and the band of states across the Midwest are bass havens, and you'll find largemouths in company with smallmouths right into the more northern states.

The best thing you can do is to master the uses of all your bass-fishing gear. Learn to spot-cast with plugs and spoons so that you can land that lure on a dime. It will save a lot of hang-ups. Do not be afraid to lose or snag a lure. It is better to risk a good strike from a spot where you feel you might get hung up than to bypass it and go home fishless. Tackle is expendable, but time on the water is not. We are all thankful for those hours spent on the water in our pursuit of fishing happiness. What's a few lost lures?

The most important rule of thumb is to keep alert to all the signs. These can come from the natural surroundings, but quite often they come from the mouths of fishermen when their arms are bent over fishing-tackle counters. You'll learn the hows and wheres from conversations in local taverns, local rod and gun clubs and at the bait and boat liveries. You can also watch how the other fishermen are doing on the lake. A pair of binoculars can often reveal what many books will never show you. Quite a few fishermen who never wrote or read a book know more than any of us about how to catch bass on their particular lake. While all basic methods and tackle arrangements will take bass at one time or other, it is of prime importance to find out what is happening in the local scene in which you find yourself. If you can.

What I showed you in our jaunt after the pickerel will work well in your bass fishing. Learn to scan the lake and get the *feel* of the shoreline, and seek out the places in that lake which will offer you the best chances of success.

Remember that the good bass fisherman is first a good bass hunter. Trial and error over the years will bring forth opinions as to where to fish and with what.

One way to save a lot of time in hunting is to get a geodetic map of the countryside and study the depth lines of the lake. If you cannot come by a geodetic map, publications from the state conservation departments are full of lake and stream maps which will show you enough to get started. Again, watch where the locals fish, particularly when they are working the deep parts of the lake, for they know the spring holes where the bass go in the hot weather. While those bass are down deep, they are not necessarily on the feed. They rest there during the day and forage in toward the shore or the midlake shallows during the night. Troll with the best of the talent, for they are out hunting with you.

What is said here about largemouth-bass fishing applies equally to the search for action from the smallmouth.

Lures come in many colors. I have never yet been able to ascertain just what colors appeal most to the bass at particular times and under certain conditions. At night I use an all-black plug, since I believe that the black silhouette is easier for them to see. The fisherman in a boat upshore will be using a red and white plug at night, and it is likely that he'll come in with just as many bass, or just as few as I will. During the day, your choice between a green-and-white or a red-and-white plug is merely for your own satisfaction. Only a complete recording of all bass taken on all colors and the totals figured by computer would come up with a fact worth recording. But take that result out fishing with you the next day, and the bass would make that machine appear utterly useless. The perch-finish and minnow-colored plugs certainly look good on the tackle counters, and I've bought myriads of them. I've taken bass at times on all of them, and I've also taken no bass on all of them. But I consider a good supply of all the possibilities necessary to my own well-being and patience. If I lose patience with the bass, I can spend my energy in changing lures in order to try to confound them.

The same goes for spoons. You can use the regulation old-type spoon. Or you can use red-and-white and green-and-white daredevil, which has stood the test of time among all anglers for all types of fish, both fresh- and saltwater varieties. But perhaps the reason why spoons kill so many fish is because so many fishermen fish with them. I'm being frank here, as honest as any angler can be. I do not push coincidence and try to make it into fact because this has confounded me too many times. Arm yourself well and by some sort of magical guidance, you'll fish with the right lure enough times, or it may be that the lure itself doesn't make as much difference as the tackle manufacturers

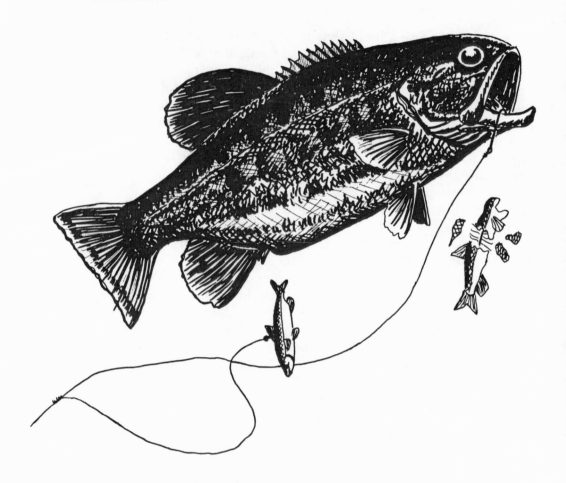

would have you think. I do believe, however, that the fisherman who knows just how to manipulate a lure so that it becomes a living threat or an enticing bit of food to the bass is the one who consistently catches more bass than most others.

Master your tackle well so you can push its potentialities to the very limit. When you start to find yourself limited in your casting, you can buy better equipment that really works for you: a proper reel that functions smoothly and effortlessly in your hand, a rod that answers your every response and lures that literally come to life when you manipulate them. These are the extras that the experts develop and part of the reason why they seem to catch more bass than the rest of us.

Smallmouth Bass

The smallmouth has all the characteristics of the largemouth and shows a lot more fierceness in striking and fighting ability, at the same time being trickier, or at least more particular. He's not nearly as easy to catch, even under the best conditions.

What you learn in largemouth fishing you must strive to improve for the best results with this magnificent American fish.

One way to go after him is to know your lures and their actions. Most fishermen cast too much in too many places, retrieve their lures much too fast and then move on to supposedly greener pastures. They miss a lot of bass.

One way to get started is to know the action that has been built into the lures you are using. A few minutes spent watching a new plug will tell you all about it and its potentialities. Retrieve it from the very slowest action to the fastest and remember what you are seeing. There are times when bass will take only an extremely slow-moving lure. Other times they'll spirit your fastest retrieve. I learned this lesson one night when I had been trolling a surface plug well behind the boat. We had stopped to cast a bit, and I left the plug floating out there, well behind us. When I started up the motor, we took off fairly quickly and when we were well underway, a bass actually took that plug. According to all the rules, we were going much to fast for him. Just what he thought it was, or why it appealed to him to the point of straining his every fin, I'll never know. But ne took that plug, and it was such a shock that the rig almost bounced out of the boat.

Shown in the diagram below are the three basic lure actions. The first [A] is the surface-popping plug. On the retrieve it zigzags or wobbles, kicking up a fuss on the surface. Use this kind when the water is glassy calm. Pause as indicated several times on the retrieve. Do not retrieve it too fast and remember that the designer put action into it for specific speeds. Milk his

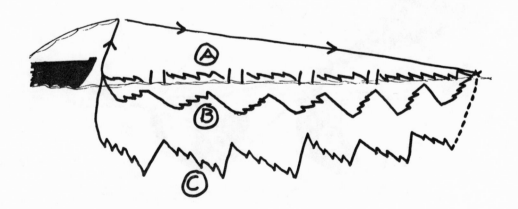

invention to the utmost! The next [B] is the floating-diving-wobbling plug action. This is started by pulling and causes descending to the degree of your speed of retrieve. To make it dive, pull back on the rod tip and retrieve at the same time. When you pause, it will float back up toward the surface. Dive it again by a fast retrieve, governing your depth by the depth of the water in which you are fishing. In [C] we have the diving, wobbling plug that sinks when you let up the pressure and rises when you make the retrieve. Study these diagrams and then give your plugs a practice run where you can see their action and just how they move about under specific speeds. You can govern your trolling speeds accordingly.

In all fishing, anglers like to go out with partners. Two people fishing at the same time, using different lures, can cut down the experimental times and arrive at a killing lure or retrieve or trolling speed.

But, in a small boat, two anglers who are both casting can offer some danger unless they watch what they are doing. Shown below is the best possible and safest way of working together. Seated this way and recognizing their boundaries of casting space so that they will not hook each other, they can both cast at the same time without a tangle.

It is quite often profitable for both anglers to switch positions in the boat. It is a bit unfair for the skipper to always handle the motor and also be in the second position. A safe way to switch positions is shown below in two steps. Remember this and

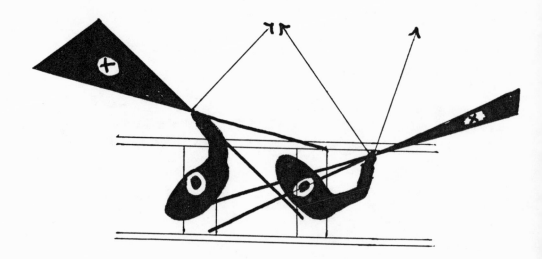

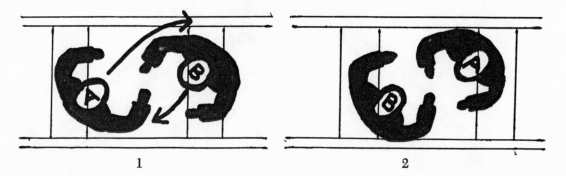

1   2

practice it at the dock. Two people in a small boat can easily
capsize it if they both move in the wrong directions and throw
their weight in the same quarter at the same time.

Most anglers retrieve and also troll too fast. Make it a practice
to take it easy. Also try not to cast too many times, too often, in
the same place. Pause a bit. If you are sure, for instance, that
there is a bass in there by that windfall and in front of the rock,
place the first cast well outside and the second to the left, and the
next one to the right. Pause, change lures and repeat the process.

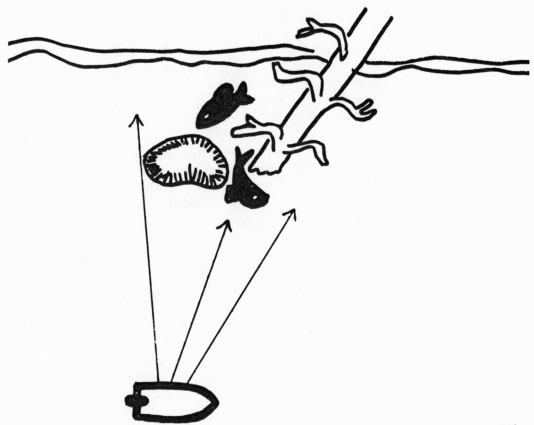

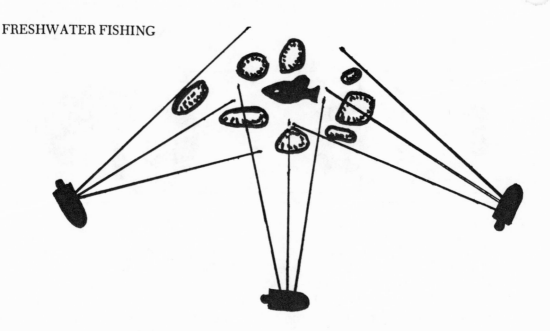

A change of direction is always a good measure. Suppose you are fishing a rock cluster and a bass is in there. Work your casts from one angle and then, changing the lure, cast at him from another, hitting the same spots as before.

While all manner of live baits are good for smallmouth-bass fishing, I like to use the hellgrammite, shown below, when I can catch them or buy them at the bait dealers. I merely hook them through the tail section or under the collar, being careful not to kill the insect by penetrating into the body. This makes a potent fly-rod lure that can easily be cast to fair distances with the big rod. If you try not to flip the bait too strongly on the back cast, you won't flick it off. Fish it like a wet fly or moving bucktail, slowly retrieving and giving it motion via jiggling the rod tip. Let it pause a few times during the retrieve. All game fish love it, so you are liable to catch most any species with it.

Some of the best smallmouth-bass water in the United States never had any bass there until they were planted. Years ago, the fishermen in northern Maine were witnessing the decline of the brook trout in the lakes and connecting streams. When the smallmouth bass were put in there, they thrived. The Grand Lake Stream section of Maine is now one of the top areas for smallmouth fishing. At the other end of the map, the state of Washington has good supplies of them, especially in the lakes. You can fish for cutthroat trout in the centers of these lakes and then go ashore, casting or trolling along the shoreline, and take energetic smallmouth bass that will consistently go four and five pounds and even larger.

Stream and River Smallmouths

The stream and river smallmouths are the delight of anglers who fish the lower reaches of some of the famous trout streams in the East that are located in Pennsylvania, New York and New England. These river smallmouths make the same weight trout look sick. They will sock a dry fly meant for a trout and give you a real tussle. Bass bugs of small size, and big dry flies such as the Wulff pattern shown here are prime favorites.

These are for the fast streams and boulder-strewn rapids and pool tops. The broad, slower rivers also contain good smallmouth-bass populations. Regulation spinning tackle and trolling lures are fine for them, trolled either deep or on the surface.

WALLEYED PIKE

The walleye, commonly called the pike perch, will fight you with less intensity than a big panfish and yet more ferociously than a smallish game fish. His extra weight makes him a heavier fighter and stronger puller on tackle than smaller fish, but he's nowhere near the buster that the pike of the same weight is.

He's strictly a bait eater, seldom if ever feeding on flies, so you'll lure him with spinners and bait, spoons, jigs, trolled spinners and bait plugs.

He's a school fish and he gangs up with his fellow walleyes mainly in the spring and fall, spending the summer in the deepest parts of the lake. This tells that we can catch him on lures when he is on the move, or by still-fishing and deep trolling in the summer when he is down deep.

He is called a walleye because his eyeball is milky white, giving the impression that he is almost totally blind. This is far from the case.

Let's fish for him. We can learn from the local fishermen just where the hot spots are on the lake or, by trolling, we can locate our own and mark them as shown here in the diagram.

Depending on the temperature of the lake and the season of the year, we can determine the best areas to troll by studying a

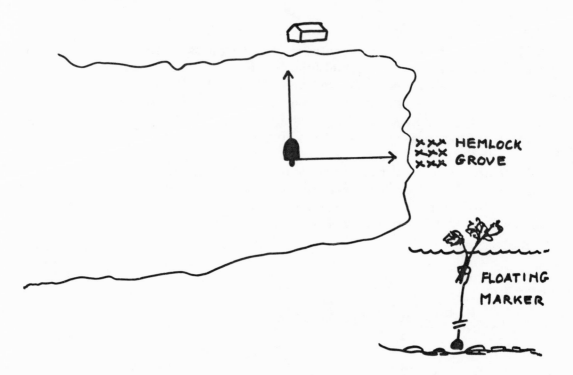

XXX HEMLOCK
XXX GROVE

FLOATING MARKER

contour map of the lake. If our lake looks like the one below with the temperature bands as indicated (walleyes like temperatures about sixty degrees, as a general rule), we can easily determine our course.

We'll use a bait rig borrowed from the pike and muskie fishermen and troll it. Drift it down deep with a very little weight or really sink it down quickly.

Once the general temperature reading is established for specific depths, a regulation depth map can be used for reference.

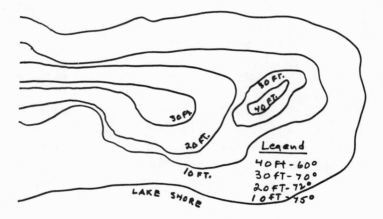

30 FT.
40 FT.
30 FT.
20 FT.
10 FT.

Legend
40 FT - 60°
30 FT - 70°
20 FT - 72°
10 FT - 75°

LAKE SHORE

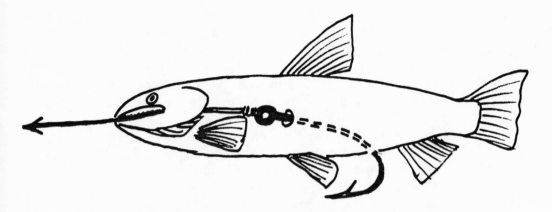

We'll pick a day that is cool and overcast, for our own benefit. No one likes to bake in the sun if it is not necessary.

Since these fish are ravenous during the spring, especially after their spawning season, we can feel assured that we will be successful with trolled lures such as sinking diving plugs, spoons or spinners-and-bait combinations, trolled at the river mouths, sandbars or midlake rock clusters. Our fishing will be done at dawn or at twilight, unless the day is overcast and the temperature is down.

Jigs of the type shown below are well-known favorites. Usually part of your saltwater tackle box, the jig has become a number one lure for walleyes and other freshwater game fish, including the basses.

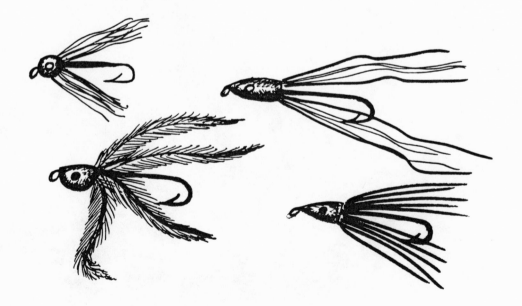

Since these jigs have no action of their own, it must be simulated by rod-tip motion and the speed of line retrieve. Bounce them over the grassy gravel bottoms in the shallows or jig them up and down when fishing the deeper sections.

Quite often a weighted jig and spoon combination is used to further entice the walleyes. Use a trolling fin ahead of the rig so that the line doesn't twist.

Incidentally, if your line becomes twisted, don't try to reel it in and untangle it as it comes. And don't try to reel it in in a mess to work on it later. Merely hand-haul the line in, take off the lure or terminal tackle and run the boat fast for about fifteen minutes with the line straight out behind the boat. This will pull and unravel the twists for you.

The strike and the fight with the walleye are not dramatic, but he does have a weight advantage. A good walleye will bend your rod and strain the reel drag. Fighting him is fun. You'll also have a good meal, for Midwesterners consider the walleye to be one of the tastiest of all freshwater fish.

PIKE AND MUSKIE

All that we have written about bass fishing can be applied to pike and muskie fishing. Remember also that these two magnificent battlers are going to give you the fight of your life. They are really tough, and their teeth are dangerous. A big

muskie can give you as much of a bite as a barracuda, so be careful. He will tear a landing net to pieces if you net him the wrong way.

In fishing for muskie and pike, you'll need braided metal leaders ahead of your lures. Those shown here can be bought, and you must use them.

You can also buy leaders that are plastic coated for the purpose of making them less visible in the water. But it is unnecessary, since if a pike or muskie wants that lure, he will grab it even if it's tied to a piece of rope.

These fish do not feed on flies on the surface; in fact, little of their diet contains flies. They are strictly meat eaters, feeding on the lesser fish, including whitefish, suckers, freshwater herring, smelt or whatever species happen to inhabit the lake.

The best way to rig a bait for trolling or casting is by the procedure shown in the section on walleye fishing. As with the walleye, spring and fall are the best times to find these fish in the shallows and, after spawning time in the spring, they can be found in big schools. During the summer, pike and muskie require deep trolling.

Heavy-duty tackle and extra heavy line are recommended when fishing for them in weed beds where you'll also have to battle with snags, lily-pad stems and lake rushes.

They both strike hard and mean to battle. As with the pike illustrated here, they'll body-roll most of the time, but when they hit that surface they can really throw the spray. If you can manage to stay calm and handle the line correctly when one of them jumps into the air beside the boat, the fish will still be on the hook for you.

Once he's hooked, hold your rod high in anticipation of the fish dashing under the boat or jumping into the air. As the fish draws near, loosen up on the reel drag to accommodate a sudden rush. If fishing with a partner, have him move the boat into a position that will allow a free fighting area away from snags. If

the fish runs under the boat, your partner can swing the boat sideways, exposing the fish.

Net him and you'll have the prize fish of America.

TROUT

The techniques used in fishing for brown and rainbow trout are quite similar. Those used for cutthroats and steelheads differ somewhat and have to be treated separately. All trout in lakes demand the same general tackle and lure presentation.

Trout are usually found in creeks, brooks, streams and large rivers. They are either native to these waters or have been planted there and, when possible, have since been able to reproduce and thrive as "native" fish.

Their food is essentially aquatic insects, that is, insects which live in the water, under and around the rocks, in the sand and in the stream bed. Some of these flies—mayflies, caddises and stones being three of the most common—can be represented in their underwater form by wet flies and nymphs. (See Chapter 4.)

When these insects hatch or come into their final phase of existence, they rise up through the water and open their wings in flight. Some of these insects alight on the water and drift on the currents for quite a distance. This is the time that the dry-fly fisherman can catch trout with some ease, providing that his presentation and choice of fly is the right one.

The trout's diet also includes the stream minnow, small trout and other small fish of the stream, plus, of course, the wash-ins such as earthworms and land-bred insects such as moths and grasshoppers.

So, trout can be caught with live bait, live or dead insects impaled on the hook, or with artificial flies and lures.

Light spinning gear is normally used for small-to-medium-size trout in ordinary streams. The bigger tackle is necessary for the big fish in broad, fast rivers. The fly rod, ranging from the six footer with a soft action to the nine footer with the stiff action can be used. Which one to use is determined not so much by the size of the fish but by the casting demands.

Brook trout and brown trout generally spawn in the fall. The rainbow spawns in the spring. Spring and fall are the best times to catch trout, though in many streams where the water stays cool in the summer, good trout fishing can be enjoyed all through the summer, especially in the early morning and late evening. Night fishing, where legal, is also one of the best ways to catch the big ones.

The objective in trout fishing is to wade out and then make your casts so that you will not scare the trout. These fish are especially shy to the shadow of a person wading over them. They are often found in shallow water, hardly knee deep, and so they can see you readily and dart behind a rock or into the deeper part of a pool, hiding until you go away. Scared trout are not likely to take your bait no matter how alluring, or your fly no matter how enticingly you float it over them.

The manner of presentation demands that you know your tackle, especially the fly rod, and be able to make all the different types and variations of the casts that I described in Chapter 3. Study the currents and you can see that in order to float flies in those currents you must learn how to cast the line so that the fly will not be jerked by the current. The object is to allow the fly to drift in the current and appear as natural as a drifting fly would appear. Trout are very suspicious of any unnatural movement. The art of reading the water is something you'll have to learn by experimentation. There will be times when you'll connect, when you'll catch trout after trout without any knowledge of why. Go to the same pool the next day and you'll find that the trout will not even rise to a fly, but will rest and watch for food to drift down to them from above.

In the high and cloudy water of early spring, the trout are not as selective as they are in the lower, gin-clear waters of summer. In the summer, there is more food available to them, so they will not grab your fly simply because you have cast it and presented it well to them.

Trout fishing requires patience and lots of observation. It is better to look before you wade and figure out the angles before you cast. Keep an eye on the water for the shape, size and color of the insects that are about.

Trout lie in specific places at different times during the year according to the type of stream you find them in.

When a stream is in the mountains, there are mostly fast runs and deep pools. The trout will lie under the white water at the head of a pool and at the tail of the pool if there are rocks to hide behind or under. If there is a deep section of the pool, the daytime will find the trout deep down. But when the insects begin to move in the water and hatch on the surface, a pool that you might have thought contained no trout at all will come alive, and you will see action that looks like the fish hatchery at feeding time.

The slower, broader rivers harbor trout all along the edges. You can bet that there are trout ahead of the collections of large rocks, in the vacuum of current under the slipstream, and certainly where the foam starts as the rock breaks the current flow. Here again, the central currents and deep runs will hold good fish that will nurse the bottom until the flies begin to become active. When you see the flies popping into the air over the stream, you know that there is a hatch on, and it is time to either tie two wet flies or a dry fly on a slim leader. Sometimes a wet fly can be used as a bobber fly ahead of the dry fly. These rigs are cast and fluttered over the surface either across or slightly downstream. The best angles to fish the dry fly are across-and-up or straight upstream. Note the rigs and the various methods and directions of casting in the accompanying diagrams.

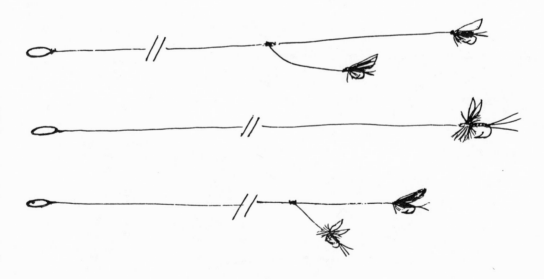

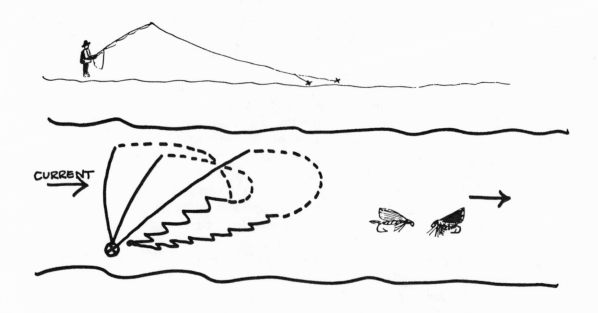

CURRENT

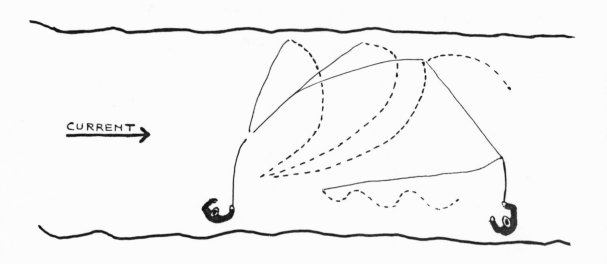

CURRENT

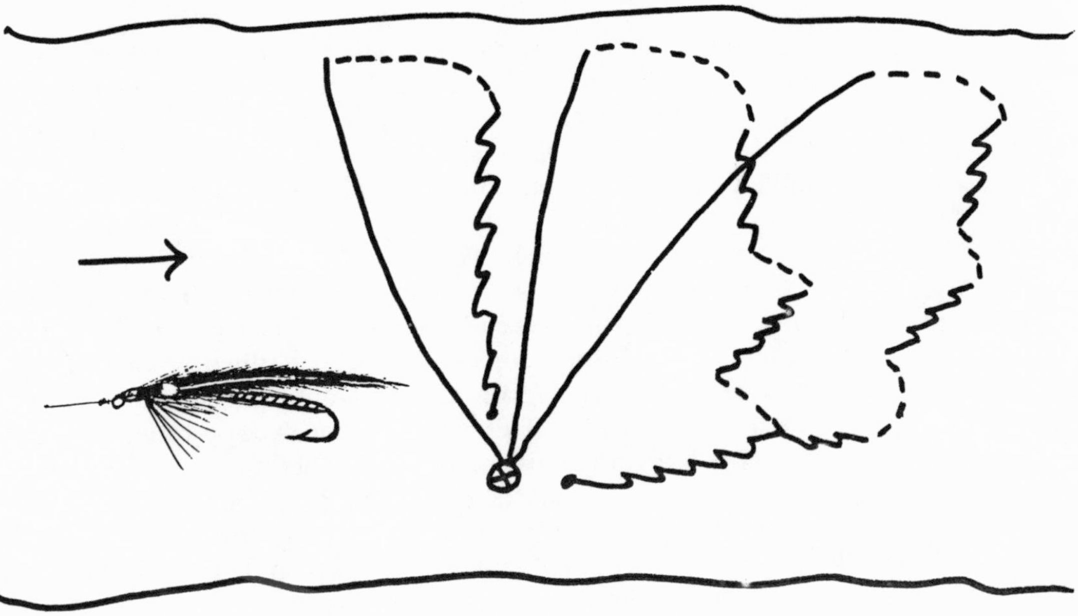

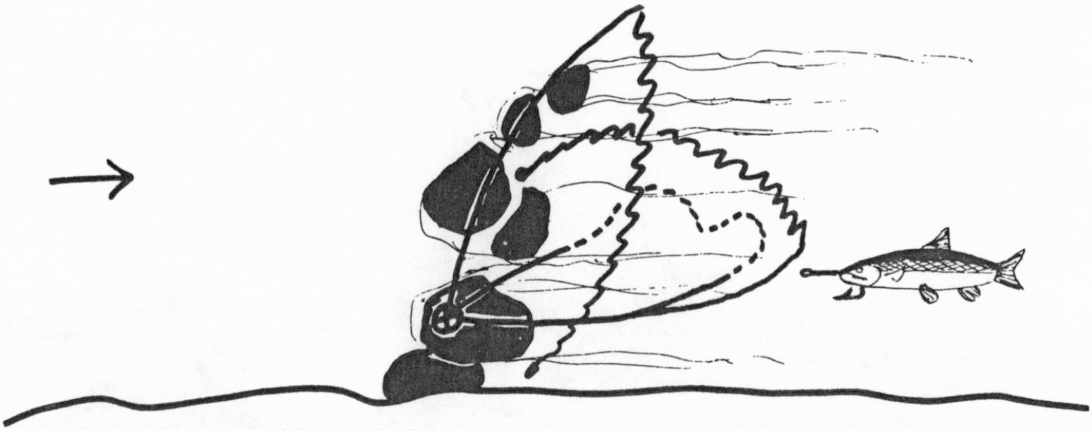

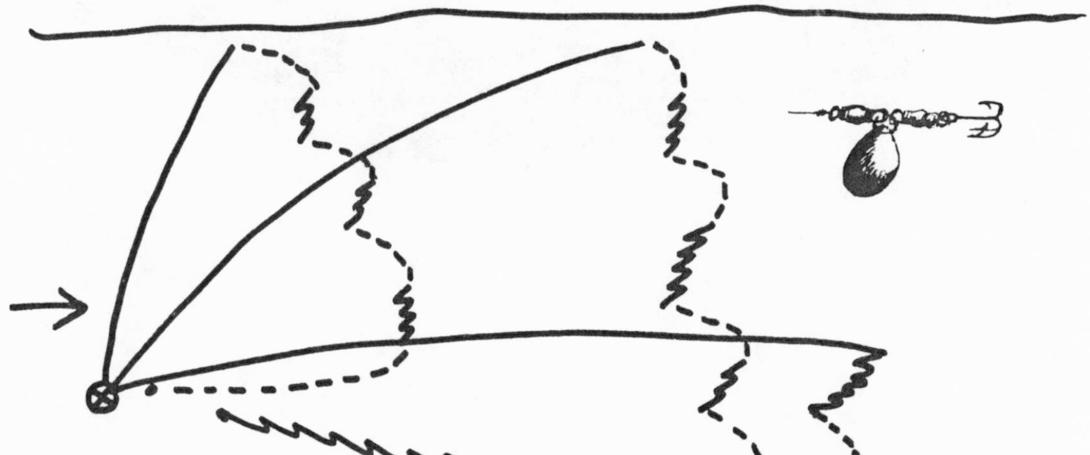

Live bait (see Chapter 4) cast either with a fly rod or a light spinning rod is placed at the head of a run, at the edge of a sunken rock or in the main wash of a current. The bait is allowed to drift down into the water as naturally as possible and then is pulled along with the current and retrieved quietly for the recast.

Spinning lures, such as the Colorado spinner and small spoons, often with a worm dangled from the hooks, are also good as long as the lures can wobble with the current.

While lake-fishing for trout you will discover one of two extremes. In the spring and fall the trout usually surface quite a bit, feeding on flies. This is dry-fly and wet-fly time, although spinning lures might also produce some action.

In the summer months trout fishing on the lakes is very difficult, and you must get down to them by trolling and by still-fishing both live bait without weights and weighted baits in combination with lures. As in all fishing, you must learn where the lake's hot spots are.

CUTTHROAT AND STEELHEAD

The west coast of North America from Los Angeles to the tip of Alaska is probably the greatest area for salmon and steelhead and cutthroat trout in the entire world. At one time, before lumbermen and pollution cut down the migrating rivers to a relative few, the waters just off the entire seacoast and the rivers that went well inland to the mountains contained hordes of salmon and their followers, the egg-eating steelhead and cutthroat trout. Today, conservation groups are taking action to try to stop the decline of these marvelous food and game fishes, as the recreational as well as the food value of them has been more widely recognized.

In general the runs of these fish follow the salmon. The winter and summer runs are geared to the migration upstream of the various species of Pacific salmon.

Winter steelheading is a cold sport, even in the northern California streams, and, often, freezing weather is encountered. During this season the two do not feed on flies. They are egg-conscious, and salmon eggs and clusters of steelhead eggs are used to bait them as shown in the diagram. To the confirmed fly-fisherman, this method seems to mean a "must miss," but if you are to tangle with a steelie, you'll have to do it this way or at best settle for far fewer strikes with the use of spoons and spinners.

The most productive areas of the big rivers to fish are at the bends and corners or where there is an obstruction in the current. These are the places where the fish congregate for their sprint up the swift currents to the next pool above. While they are on the move, they are not as easy to lure as when they are resting or circling around in comparatively quiet water away from the surging main currents of the stream.

Shown in the accompanying diagram is a portion of the stream and the spots where the angler should fish for these trout with his egg rigs set out as described in Chapter 4.

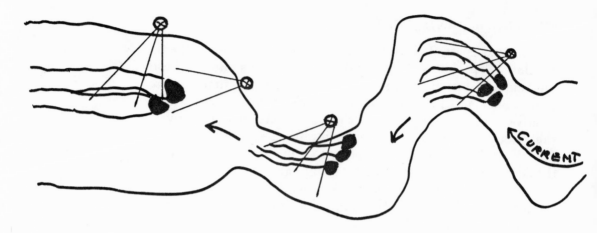

In the summertime, when the steelheads are either in or drifting back toward the ocean, they again will begin feeding on insects. It is then that the large and weighted wet flies, the streamer-bucktail creations, take good fish. Once in a while under perfect conditions, they can be taken on big dry flies. When this happens, the angler can consider himself lucky. It may not happen again for a long time.

Steelheading demands good strong tackle, because you will be casting heavy and bulky baits and big spoons and spinning lures. Since your casting and fishing will be largely downstream, a hooked fish will not be easy to land. The best procedure is to situate yourself below the fish, or wait until he heads upstream, and then get out in shallow water and gradually work him to the shallows into an already submerged net. Take along a large net, because the steelhead is big and long and jumps like his big brother the Atlantic salmon. And his meat is sweet!

Cutthroat fishing on lakes is a lot of fun and not too tricky. When I was stationed at Ft. Lewis, I was able to fish fifty lakes within a day's run of the fort. Most of them produced cutthroat weighing as much as four pounds, and casting for them with light tackle and light surface trolling afforded great sport. I also took a good many cuts from the brooks and streams that branched out from the saltwater near Seattle. Out on the Olympic Peninsula, I had my best steelhead and cutthroat angling, measuring by numbers of fish. But I'll still remember the beauty of the first really big steelhead that I took from the Eel River in California amidst the towering redwoods. The fish was only a part of the scene, but the whole experience has stuck with me since the very instant of landing that big fish.

SALMON

Landlocked Salmon

The landlocked salmon is a fish with a very limited range, but if you are ever fortunate enough to get to its waters, you'll have the battle of your life, even if the fish is small. I've taken one pounders that could make a three-pound rainbow look and act like a guppy. I've never seen a fish jump around on the surface in a series of tail walks like the landlock. He's simply out of this world. Take him on light tackle, as I have taken them, and you have fifteen minutes of terror! Troll for them with the tandem-hooked streamers. The reason for this particular fly is that it imitates their most natural food, the smelt, and various herring or whitefish that their lake affords. They will take spinners and worms if they are feeding well on the surface, and once in a while you can take them on large wet flies cast on the surface or skip-trolled across the top. The best place to take them is at the mouth of a brook or stream that enters the lake. The best time is when it is still cold, just after the ice has gone out of the lake. They feed on the surface for a few weeks and then descend to the bottom of the lake for the remainder of the year. After those first few weeks, you can take them in the early morning, on a very cloudy day or at eventide by trolling the surface. Fall is also a good time of year, for again they come back to the top.

Standard trolling procedures are called for. Spinners, spoons, long slim plugs and tandem streamer flies are the best lures.

I've taken a few on dry flies at the mouth of brooks in the early spring, but this type of fishing is not standard procedure.

Atlantic Salmon

The Atlantic salmon is judged to be the king of all freshwater fishes, and I'm not one to argue. He makes the best fly-fishing in this hemisphere.

They ascend the big streams of the Northeast, and casting has to be done with long rods, of at least nine feet for best and longest cast results. You can take them on rods of six feet in length with regulation-size trout tackle, but it will take a few years of experience to perform that feat.

Be prepared for a magnificent leap the second that the salmon feels the barb of your hook. He doesn't generally strike hard unless the fly is on a swing in the current or he takes it as you are retrieving the line. Often merely a bump on your line signifies a take. Sometimes, if the fly is drifting slack as it should, you don't even feel him take it. But once he's on, you are in for anywhere from fifteen minutes to a half hour of battling to tire him out.

Actually, Atlantic salmon fishing is quite simple, far simpler than trout fishing. I've seen people catch big salmon who have never fished before. One day, on the Miramichi River in New Brunswick, I saw a ten-year-old boy cast to the salmon the first time he had ever held a rod. He didn't even know how to manage the tackle, but he learned quickly.

There are some subtleties, of course, but these are designed for the angler, not the fish. As for sporting value, the Atlantic salmon will give you more than you bargained for in brute strength, fast clipping runs, acrobatic surface lunges and clear skyward leaps.

Learn to know your fly-rod tackle and just how far your leader will stretch. Be able to cast well into a strong wind and be strong of leg to wade the deep and fast currents you'll need to walk in during your trip for salmon. You can fish for salmon from the bow seat in a canoe with a guide who will put you over the fish. Fishing from the shore is also possible on most salmon pools.

The season for salmon generally begins in May, but the best runs are in September and the beginning of October. The salmon ascends the streams and takes his time going up according to the dryness of the season. A prolonged dry spell might keep the fish at the mouth of the river for a month, and after the first rains, the river will be filled with them in every pool and run. Fishing for them is a gamble since finding them can be difficult.

Big wet flies, small wets, trout-size wets and nymphs take them, but the dry fly is the epitome of the art.

It would be quite foolhardy to attempt to fish for salmon without a guide unless you have had years of experience and know of rivers where you can fish alone. Most waters are controlled by guides, outfitters and camps. A guide can save you a lot of aggravation as well as be there to help you and net your fish for you.

Of all the kinds of fishing, going after the Atlantic is the most expensive in terms of guide charges, resort charges and the like. But it is well worth the price.

Pacific Salmon

For the most part, the various species of Pacific salmon are taken in the saltwater close to and at mouths of rivers, and upstream into the brackish water. They are trolled for and cast to with heavy spoons and spinner rigs. When fishing well upriver, the angler uses lighter tackle, though of sufficient back-bone and resistance, to cast heavy lures into very fast and deep water.

It is imperative for you to contact a good guide and boatman if you are to really connect. The conditions of the particular moment are of utmost importance in this type of fishing—the time of year, the water conditions, the lures needed and the whereabouts of the fish schools.

You'll learn all you need to know about this kind of salmon fishing from the guides and outfitters. As usual, visit the tackle stores and bone up a bit on what's new for salmon angling.

SHAD

Found on both coasts, the shad is an anadromous fish, ascending the rivers and creeks from Nova Scotia to Florida and from northern California to British Columbia. It is a member of the herring family, very soft mouthed, and feeds on small flies and possibly minnows. They take minnowlike lures, small glittering spinning lures and tinsel-bodied wet flies. My favorite is the silver Colorado spinner. Try for them at the pools, because they seldom take while on the run along the regular river pattern. Light-to-medium spinning gear and fly rods are recommended.

MOST POPULAR 9
GAME FISH SPECIES

There are approximately fifty species of fish above the size of the minnow in the freshwater of North America. However, we are concerned here with only the principal game and food fishes. These two terms, *game* and *food*, often overlap, since all game species are also good food fishes. There are, however, some food fishes that are not considered "sporty" to catch. Listed, described and illustrated in this chapter are the most popular fish, those that have won their place in anglers' hearts ever since Americans began to fish. Exactly what constitutes a game fish remains debatable, since, with the perfection of ultralight fishing rigs, even the sluggish catfish can give you quite a fight.

Since there are so many popular names given to fish, the Latin identification is included with the illustrations.

A diagram of a typical fish (bass) is shown here with the parts identified.

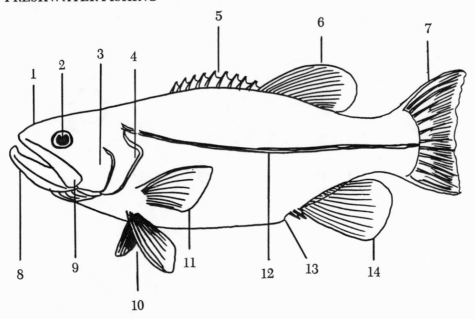

TYPICAL FISH

This is a diagram of a typical fish with the principal parts labeled as shown: *1]* Snout. *2]* Eye. *3]* Cheek. *4]* Gill cover. *5]* Spinous portion of dorsal fin. *6]* Soft portion of dorsal fin. *7]* Caudal fin. *8]* Mandible or lower jaw. *9]* Maxillary. *10]* Ventral fins. *11]* Pectoral fins. *12]* Lateral line (sense organs). *13]* Anus. *14]* Anal fin.

TROUTS (Chars and Salmonoids)

The waters of the northern states from Maine to Washington contain trout, with the possible exception of the plains states, where there are few mountain lakes and cold-water streams, and, of course, the desert areas. Trout can live in aerated streams and deep cold lakes as far south as Georgia, Arkansas, Arizona and Southern California, but they range toward the colder regions of the country. In high altitudes farther south, conditions are also favorable for them. Look for trout in lakes and streams where the water temperature ranges from above freezing to around seventy-two degrees Fahrenheit. Trout can seldom withstand actual freezing temperatures and none can

live in water higher than seventy-five degrees unless it is exceptionally well aerated.

All three methods—spinning, fly-fishing and bait casting—are used to catch trout. Live bait such as minnows, worms and aquatic insects are taken readily by them as well as their artificial counterparts in the form of artificial flies, spinners, spoons, plugs and all variations of these lure types.

Brook Trout [Salvelinus fontinalis]

The brook trout is a native of the Eastern states and a favorite of the fisherman. Since earliest days, the brookie or "squaretail" has been planted in many Western waters where it has thrived even better than in its original habitat. It is judged to be the prettiest of all trout. It is a char, not a salmon-colored fish as are most of the others. The bright red-orange fins, highlighted by a black and white front-fin set of stripes are not found on any other species except the lake trout, which is a close cousin. The olive green back is worm-marked with dark brownish mackerel-like streaks. The trout's sides have light blue spots with rose red centers.

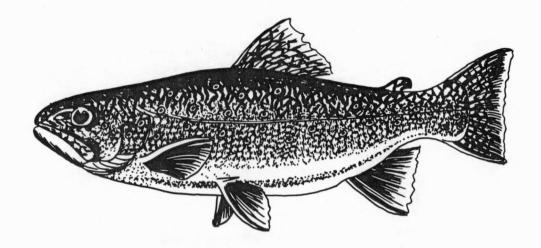

The average brook-trout size varies with the waters and conditions, but the largest weigh from two to four pounds. The fish of the creeks seldom weigh over a half pound.

The best time of the year to catch brookies is in the spring, after the ice breaks up in the lakes and the initial runoff of high waters in the streams and creeks is past. Brookies, like all other trout, prefer minnows, worms and aquatic insects such as the caddis and mayfly as their diet. For the sportiest methods of catching them use the light fly rod or the ultralight spinning rods.

If you wanted to fish for the brook trout in his original home, the Northeast, you might fish in one of the New England states. Here the streams are cold and clear. The ice leaves the lakes in late April, and from then until the hot days of summer, brook-trout fishing in the lakes and streams is superb. Worms are the best bait, though small spinning lures are often excellent. The traditional wet flies and streamers are effective most of the time.

If you were fishing a large river, you might be guided by an old woodsman poling or paddling you in a canoe up or down the river, stopping at favorite deep holes where the trout lie. You could also wade the streams, cold as they may be, and cast carefully into the pockets and deep dark spots along the stream edges. In lake fishing early morning and twilight are the best times. The water is calm and quiet then. The trout will come up at such times to feed on insects and small minnows, and you cast to them with flies and small lures.

Brook trout are found as far west as Michigan and Ontario. They grow big in northern Canada and are at their largest in

Newfoundland and Labrador. During the past fifty years they have been successfully stocked in streams where the temperature seldom exceeds seventy degrees. They thrive in the Rockies and on the northern West Coast. They do not rise as avidly to the dry fly as the brown trout or rainbow. Their fight is a strong body roll rather than a long leap or fast run, such as the rainbow makes. Brook trout are treasured for their unusual colors and excellent pink meat that seems to melt in your mouth. Fish for them with fly-fishing tackle or spinning gear, the lighter the better.

Brown Trout [Salmo trutta, s. fario]

The brown trout were brought from Germany in 1880 and stocked into the streams of the states of Pennsylvania and New York. They thrive in the deeper parts of good brook-trout streams and in many cases have replaced the brook trout in streams that warm up in the summertime. They are avid risers to floating insects because they will lie in large expanses of open water where the brook trout would never venture.

The brown trout grows to almost twice the size of the brook trout, especially in the lakes. Ten pounders are not too uncommon in the lakes and four pounders are taken quite often in the big rivers.

Once despised by the gentleman angler as a commoner among such as the princely brook trout, fishermen are now thankful for the brown. They fight hard in a combination of surface thrashing and body-rolling. They will also leap into the air when hooked, though not nearly as much as the rainbow trout.

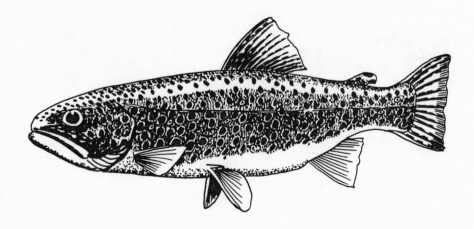

Less colorful than the brook trout, they are equals on the dining-room table to both the brook and the rainbow. Like all trout the brown will take bait, especially worms and live minnows. The height of the art of trout fishing is being able to take them on dry flies daintily cast on the flat pools of the famed trout streams of the East, such as the Beaverkill in Sullivan County, New York, the trout-fishing mecca of America.

Rainbow Trout [Salmo gairdnerii]

Before the advent of extensive transplant stocking, the rainbow trout was only caught on the West Coast and in the Mountain states. The rainbow is an anadromous fish, living part of its life in the ocean and the rest of the time, particularly during its spawning run, in streams and lakes. In most of the western Mountain states it does not have access to the ocean, so it travels up and down streams, and from lakes up into the feeder streams, following its migratory inclinations.

The rainbow is noted for its spirited leaps for flies and in response to being hooked. A running fighter rather than a body roller such as the brown and the brook trout, it often takes considerable line from light tackle in its quick dash for freedom.

Like all the species of true salmon-trout, the rainbow is a fast-water fish, brilliantly colored with blue silver on the lateral line with a deep orange-pink stripe. Black, pepperlike spots adorn the fish from nose to tail. Its belly is pink and silver tinged with some yellow. A big rainbow in a deep Western lake might reach

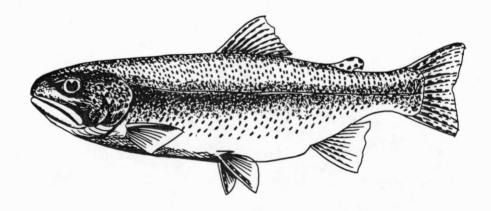

forty or fifty pounds, but they usually average less than ten pounds. Rainbows of four and six pounds are average fare for the bigger fast-running rivers and large streams.

All manner of tackle may be used, the sportiest being dry flies, wet flies, streamers and bucktails and the ultralight spinning lures. Rainbows are easily taken on bait such as worms and minnows, especially in the spring after they have spawned and are hungry.

Rainbows can now be found in good company with brown and brook trout following their first transplants from Western Coastal waters. Their famed pink red stripe, dramatic leap and tendency to run hard make them a favored prize for the angler. Taken on spinning gear or a fly rod, they offer the most active and dramatic fight of the three trout coming from a heritage that includes the migratory instinct of the salmon. They are geared for traveling up fast streams and leaping over falls to the spawning runs.

They have characteristics of a miniature salmon. They feed avidly on aquatic insects as do the other species. They are also particularly fond of bait fish.

In their native West they are the top game fish, exceeded only by their brother the steelhead trout which actually is a sea-run rainbow.

Cutthroat Trout [Salmo clarki]

The cutthroat trout has not experienced the expansion of its domain by hatchery distribution such as that enjoyed by the

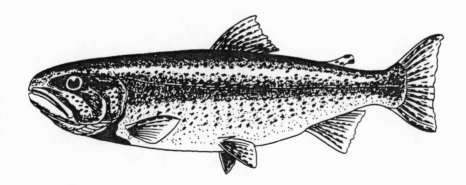

rainbow. I could never understand the reason for this other than the fact that, like the steelhead, the cutthroat follows the salmon in the migration to the spawning grounds and eats the eggs that are swept away from the salmon nest. The cutthroat is not generally considered as much of a fighter as the rainbow, though my personal experience has found them almost the same. Although they are migratory, in most other respects they are similar in habits to the rainbow. The only difference in the markings is the red slash mark that looks as if it was painted on just behind the lower side of the gills. Neither the rainbow nor any other trout species has this particular marking.

This fish does not attain the heavy weight or size of the rainbow, generally weighing in the neighborhood of fifteen pounds when taken in lakes and big rivers and two to six pounds when found in rivers and streams. They are fished for mostly in the coastal streams of northern California, Oregon and Washington and inland as far as Idaho and Wyoming in company with Dolly Varden trout.

They are not as apt to take a fly as the rainbow, but once hooked will put up a grand battle.

Dolly Varden Trout [Salvelinus malma]

The Dolly Varden trout looks just like a larger brook trout and has the same colors.

This particular trout is just beginning to go through the transplanting that the rainbow has gone through. Recent plantings in the East have proven successful. Its basic range is the Intermountain West and north into Canada where it grows to prodigious size. It is at its best in cold, clear mountain lakes and large rivers. Twenty pounders are not uncommon. It does not take a fly with the regularity of the other trouts, preferring bait and spoons and spinners of good size. Its color varies from greenish blue to a more usual bronze marked by well-spaced black dots, much larger than those found on the rainbow. It is a voracious fish, striking hard and battling well. The best technique for catching it in lakes is by trolling, and in rivers, by trolling or slow casting with drifting baits such as worms or minnows.

The Dolly is not illustrated since it essentially looks similar to the brook trout.

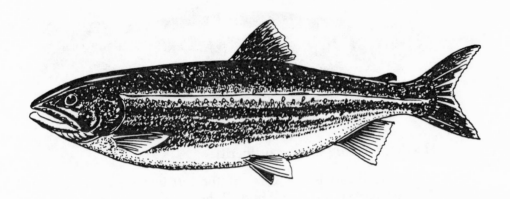

Lake Trout [Salvelinus namaycush]

From the lakes in the wilderness of Maine to the Great Lakes of the northern Midwest, the lake trout is a popular food and game fish. You catch him by trolling and still-fishing with the baits down deep. He is an active fighter but, due to the weight of the tackle used for trolling, the weight of the lures and the depth at which the fish begins its fight, the battle is not as dramatic as with the jumping rainbows that take tiny flies from the surface.

Its most distinguishing characteristic is its forked tail, which differs from the "square tail" of the brookie. Its markings are generally the same, lacking some of the pink and red spots of the brookie. The fins are duller in color.

Lakers feed on minnows, smelt, herring and a generous diet of the young whitefish that inhabit those lakes. They are best caught in the spring, but are readily available in the colder spring holes of the lakes as the season progresses. They have been transplanted far from their natural habitat and are found almost all over the Northern states and into Canada, as far north as Alaska. In the colder months they move into shallower water and in winter offer excellent ice fishing for those willing to brave the high winds and low temperatures.

Spinners and spoons with baited hooks have proven to be the most successful lures. Lake trout only come near enough to the surface of lakes to take flies or even shallow-trolled lures immediately after the ice melts.

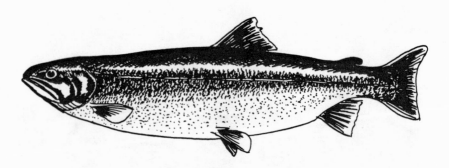

Steelhead Trout [Salmo gairdnerii]

The steelhead is the prize of the fast-water streams of the Pacific Coast states. You'll find all the rivers and creeks from San Francisco to Alaska filled with this fish almost all season long. There has always been considerable argument as to whether the steelhead is the same fish as the rainbow which it resembles very closely. It is generally concluded that they may have been at one time. The behavioral difference is that the steelhead migrates to the ocean for most of the year, ascending the freshwater streams only to spawn.

There are winter, spring, summer and fall runs of these fish in the coastal streams, varying with the location. So the visiting angler can have good sport with them in a variety of ways using all kinds of tackle and gear. Though some steelhead may reach fifty pounds, the general run in the average stream will weigh ten pounds or under.

In the winter they can be taken with salmon-egg clusters or single salmon eggs or their imitations. In the summer conventional flies and lures will do very well. Taking the steelhead on the dry fly is the supreme thrill in fly-fishing equaled perhaps only by the battle with the Atlantic salmon. They are silver blue and mother-of-pearl with a red, rainbowlike center strip that becomes brighter the longer they live in freshwater. A darker-colored steelhead has lived longer in the river than a lighter one.

SALMON

Pacific Salmon

There are five species of Pacific Salmon and all of them are excellent game and food fishes. They spend most of their year in the ocean, ascending the freshwater streams only to spawn.

The Chinook [*Oncorhynchus tshawytscha*] is the largest and

most fished for by sportsmen. It is taken in the sea and at the mouths of rivers and streams generally by spoons, spinners, and the like. It seldom if ever is caught on artificial flies. Fifty pounders are often found, but the Chinook averages around twenty to thirty. That's a lot of salmon for the freezer!

The coho [*Oncorhynchus kisutch*], also called silver salmon, is the best fly-fish in the group according to the experts and is taken in freshwater more regularly than the Chinook. He's a bit smaller, averaging around ten pounds. The sockeye [*Oncorhynchur nerka*] is only fair as a fly-rod fish but is taken on spoons and spinners in the ocean and inlets and in the larger streams and rivers. The chum [*Oncorhynchus keta*] is also only fair as a fly-fish and is found in landlocked bodies of water. Pink salmon [*Oncorhynchus gorbuscha*] is rated the least challenging to fish for in the group but is still fun to catch and good to eat.

All three methods of fishing are employed, but fly-fishing is the least productive since these salmon prefer heavier lures such as spoons and spinners and seldom feed on insects or small bait fish. Sometimes as many as three species can be found in the same place when the runs are on, making your day full of surprises.

The Pacific salmon is not illustrated because it is quite similar in shape and color to the Atlantic salmon, but it takes on a deeper red hue as it ascends the stream to spawn.

Atlantic Salmon [Salmo salar]

The Atlantic is the only salmon species found on the East Coast of North America. It is also found growing to great size in Northern Europe. Unlike the Pacific salmon, which dies on its first runs, the Atlantic salmon makes many trips to and from the

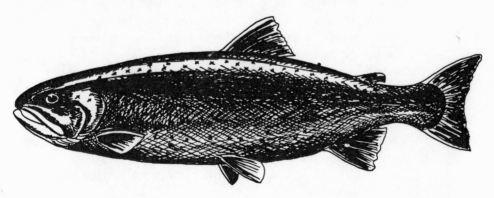

spawning rivers. It is probably the most prized sport fish of the world.

At one time the Atlantic salmon was found far to the south of its present range, but it is now limited to northern Maine rivers, throughout eastern Canada into Newfoundland and Labrador. Unlike fishing for Pacific species, the only way to catch this salmon is by fly-fishing. Authorities disagree as to whether it feeds at all in freshwater. Some believe that on its upstream migration it reverts to the habits of its early developmental stages when it would feed exclusively on insects before migrating downstream to the ocean.

The kingly Atlantic salmon is known for its majestic leaps, often numbering as many as twenty during a battle with an angler. It is built to ascend strong currents, waterfalls, and rapids, and so its strength is seemingly endless. Its meat is considered as one of the finest treats in the world. The average salmon runs from fifteen to twenty pounds but it can weigh as much as forty pounds.

Landlocked Salmon [Salmo salar sebago]

Authorities seem to agree that the landlocked salmon is a subspecies of the Atlantic variety, having been landlocked since the ice ages. With its route to the sea cut off, it has learned over thousands of years to migrate from lakes up into feeder streams. Its range is limited to the northeastern United States and eastern Canada. Transplanting of the species has never been successful elsewhere.

Fishing for landlocked salmon is best in the early spring when the ice begins to drift out in the lakes. For fly- and lure fishing the best locations are at the mouths of streams. You can troll for the fish throughout the season, particularly when the water gets warm in the late spring and summer. The fall weather makes the water cooler, and the fish are then taken near the surface by fly casting and trolling specially designed feathered streamer flies.

smaller, seldom weighing over ten pounds. Despite their lack of size, they exhibit tremendous energy in long, fun-spirited, surface battles and sensational leaps into the air.

When cooked, they taste like Atlantic salmon, but their meat is a trifle sweeter.

The landlocked salmon is a bit plumper than the Atlantic salmon. It is not illustrated here.

BASS

Smallmouth Bass [Micropterus dolomieu]

The smallmouth bass can be readily distinguished from the largemouth by the fact that the upper lip does not extend to the back of the eye. It is generally a slimmer fish than the largemouth and more bronze in color, though often the two fish cannot be distinguished from one another by color if taken from the same general location. The smallmouth is found in rivers and lakes in the Northern states where the largemouth cannot live because of lower temperatures. They are found together in most Central states areas. While the smallmouth does not grow to the size of the largemouth, averaging from two to eight pounds, it is a far more intense fighter, pound for pound putting up a more ferocious fight than any of the trouts. Both species take surface fly-rod bugs, spinning and bait-casting plugs, spoons and spinners, both underwater and off the surface, depending on the environmental conditions.

Bass are hooked from late spring to late fall. They are not a migrating fish like some of the trout but tend to hold to a specific location in a lake or stream, guarding their domain against all intruders, including anglers' lures. They can be easily provoked into striking at almost any kind of lure and tail-dancing with it across the water. They will avoid hooking onto even the treble hooks unless the angler keeps just the right amount of tension on the line. Along with the largemouth they are judged to be America's favorite game fish, and on the table, their meat is superb.

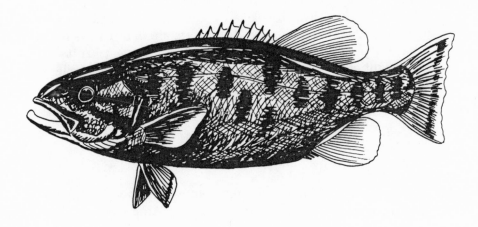

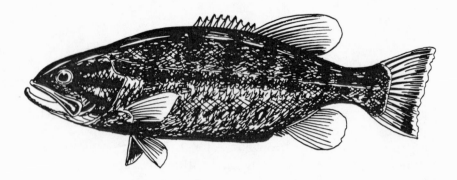

Largemouth Bass [Micropterus salmoides]

The largemouth bass is found in more areas of the country than the smallmouth, from the tip of Florida all the way to the Canadian border. In the Southern states it sometimes grows to a size of from five to fifteen pounds, but it averages from three to seven pounds in the Northern states. It is distinguished from the smallmouth physically by the fact that the upper jaw extends to a point well behind the eye. The markings and coloration are similar to the smallmouth except that it has a pronounced grouping of green splotches along the lateral line. The shape of the fish is broader and fatter than the smallmouth.

It is found mostly in lakes and slow backwater streams, feeding on crayfish, minnows, flies, bugs, frogs and mice. It is a voracious feeder, guarding its nest with a devilish killing instinct. It is lined best with surface plugs, bugs and flies when the water is calm, and underwater wounded-minnow plugs, spoons and spinner-and-bait combinations either trolled or cast and fished deep. Spinning and fly-fishing can be used, though the sport really started the development of bait-casting tackle.

Both bass species spawn in the late spring and at that time they are most easily provoked by surface lures cast over the spawning beds. In some states fishing for them at this season is illegal for purposes of conservation. They are great fun to cast for at night either from the shore or from a boat drifting silently along the coves and stream inlets.

PIKE

Northern Pike [Esox lucius]

A worldwide resident, the pike is known for both its fanatical fighting ability and good taste. In North America they do not

range below the midstates and parallel the domain of the smallmouth bass. Deep, clear Northern lakes and big inlet or chain rivers are their favorite haunts. They feed on small fish, mice, birds, freshly hatched ducklings and anything that moves and looks like food. Bigger tackle is recommended than that ordinarily used in bass fishing, particularly stronger line and larger lure. Weighted surface lures cast with either bait-casting or spinning equipment are used, for the northern pike seldom take flies or bugs, thus eliminating use of the fly rod for all practical purposes.

They are the smaller cousin of the muskellunge, but are nonetheless active fighters. Their color is light greenish, blending into a bronze on their back and peppered with darker color spots. Their weight averages from two to fifteen pounds. They are every inch a tough subsurface fighter seldom leaping clear but preferring to thrash, body-roll and bulldog the surface in an effort to shake your hooks.

They master the favorite trick of all pikes. They fight well out from the rod for a while and then they will swim in close to you as if exhausted. At just the point when you think you have them licked, they explode into action and resume the battle. Usually at this point your line is somewhat slack, and that is all they need to shake loose from the hook.

Muskellunge [Esox masquinongy]

The muskellunge is the largest and most ferocious of the pike family. No fish is as fierce as the muskie from his habit of grabbing young ducklings from the surface to his ability to leap up and grab birds from overhanging tree branches. He'll take on

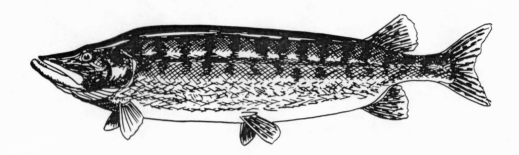

a big carp or lesser fish such as bass or trout. Often thought of as the alligator of the freshwater streams, no fish or small animal is safe when he is around.

He is found in a few Midwestern states but his main bailiwick is in the central Canadian provinces. New York State is his eastern limit, and the best waters for muskie fishing in the East is the St. Lawrence River.

He demands the strongest bait-casting tackle. Lately, many anglers are using heavy freshwater spinning gear on him, but they require heavy lines and heavy baits and the ability to set the hook hard and fast. The shorter, stiffer bait-casting rod is superior to the spinning rods ordinarily used for bass.

The biggest muskies are taken by casting or trolling large bait fish that have been harnessed with hooks in them. They are allowed to swim in the troll as naturally as possible right over the lair of the muskie. He often mouths the bait for five minutes or so, exasperating the angler into striking too soon and thus pulling the fish from his mouth. You don't get a second chance too often, for muskies are big and smart.

Chain Pickerel [Esox niger]

The baby brother of the pike family, the chain pickerel is found in lakes and ponds all across the country from Florida into the realms of the smallmouth bass and muskies. For their size they fight roughly for light tackle, but they offer good opportunities for anglers simply because they are so common, living in lakes and waters unsuitable sometimes even for the basses. They feed on minnows, frogs, crayfish and so forth.

Light spinning gear, fly rods and ultralight bait-casting rods are proper equipment for fishing pickerel, and smaller lures can be used, surface, deep-cast and trolled.

Their light greenish-brown sides blend into a white-yellow on the belly. Their characteristic chain markings of a darker color extend almost the length of the body. Their average weight is from one to five pounds.

Quite often the best place to find them is in the high grass beds along the shore or in the middle of the lakes where shallows produce thick weed growth.

While not active strikers like the bass, they can best be brought into action by patient and slow retrieves of the lure over the spots where they live or feed. They take some time to make up their minds to strike, often following the lure for some distance.

They are bony, but their meat is sweet, and they make a colorful fun-fish to battle.

Walleyed Pike [Stizostedion vitreum]

The walleye is a combination of a perch and a pike. Known also as a walleyed perch, pike perch and, in Canada, as the doré, this table delicacy shows a great amount of fighting spirit that offers one of the most satisfying catches to be found in freshwater. While they are bony, their meat is judged to be the best of all fish except the salmon. They run in size from three to about ten pounds according to their habitat.

Catching them demands a combination of still-fishing, trolling of bait, spinner-and-bait combinations and the typical

131

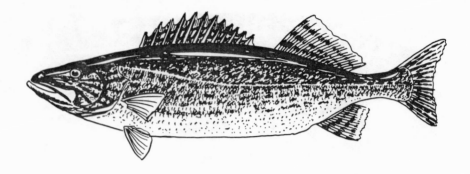

casting and trolling done in bass and pike fishing. They are primarily bait feeders and are not as a rule taken on most lures. The fly rod is seldom used.

Walleyes range over most of the northern bass, muskie, and pike areas of the country and are often found in company with them. They are much more abundant than the others, and it seems that they can never be cleared out of a given lake.

Baked walleye is a delicacy deluxe!

SHAD

American Shad [Alosa sapidissima]

The shad is similar in habits to the Atlantic salmon. It migrates from the saltwater in the spring, where it cannot be taken on lure or bait, to the spawning area far upstream. Only in freshwater will the shad strike a lure, for it, like the salmon, does not feed while on the "run."

Shad are found on both the Atlantic and the Pacific coasts and remain in freshwater for a month or so. They range from two to five pounds in weight, the hen or roe shad outweighing the buck by about two or three pounds. Shad roe, the fish's eggs, are a well-known table delicacy.

Sportsman take them on light tackle whether it be a fly rod, ultralight spinning or bait-casting stick. As they do not take bait of any kind, they can be enticed with small spinning lures, spinners and even small wet flies with tinsel on the hook shank.

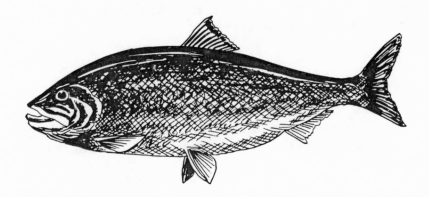

Often red and white beads strung on the hook shank will bring hefty strikes. They take a lure from annoyance or perhaps from a childhood urge. This is carried over from when they fed on small insects and tiny bait fish when they were growing big enough for the migration journey back to the sea.

Shad are a very bony fish, but this does not detract from their unusual taste on the table. There are many popular recipes by which you can cook them and dissolve all the bones.

Great care must be taken in hooking and playing shad, for their mouths are exceptionally fragile, as is that of their near cousin the herring. Play them gently but firmly and do not allow them to fight too long, or the hook will wear away a hole and they will slip off.

CATFISH AND PANFISH

Brown Bullhead [Ictalurus nebulosus]

The brown bullhead is a typical catfish of a large family and is one of the most common all over the nation. Like all cats, it is

strictly a bottom feeder, feeding exclusively on bait. He will seldom if ever hit a lure or fly. He is found in ponds, lakes and slow-moving streams and rivers.

Channel Catfish [Ictalurus punctatus]

This is the big one, weighing as much as fifty pounds in the large rivers such as the Mississippi. A bottom feeder, it takes baits of all kinds from still-fishing. Heavy gear is recommended.

Panfish (Bluegill, Crappie, Yellow Perch, White Perch, various Sunfish species)

The term *panfish* probably was tacked on to these fish simply because they fitted easily into the average frying pan. Essentially a food fish in the early days, the advent of light tackle, especially very light fly rods and ultralight spinning gear has made them popular with anglers both young and old. They are easily fooled and will take almost anything you cast at them if you can do it without scaring them away. They are usually in schools or groups in a streamside pocket or lakeshore section where there is plenty of grass and minnows for them to feed on. They are real scrappers, though not in a class with trout or bass. Panfishing is a

pleasant sport for all to enjoy, and you can do it everywhere. They are known as the backyard favorite, and good fun can be had with them without traveling hundreds of miles as with dramatic members of our large freshwater fish list.

The bluegill (above) and yellow perch (below) are illustrated here.

APPENDIXES

PLANNING YOUR FISHING TRIP

Planning can be as much fun as the actual trip itself. It can take months of detailed exploration into the area in which you are interested. This includes information concerning natural wonders, rivers, ponds, lakes, streams, rivers and oceans. Research will include letters to the local chambers of commerce, the state department of conservation, reading of regional publications, thumbing through national magazines for articles on the particular sport of each location. Then you should write to all the outfitters and resorts in the area you have selected to get their views on the possibilities, costs, dates and, also, what tackle and general outdoor equipment will be needed.

Then make your trips to the tackle stores, but remember that the lures and terminal gear had best be bought on the spot.

Have a good trip. Know your tackle and the general fishing techniques you'll need "on location." Take this book along with you for ready reference.

Included at the back of this book is a list of information sources you should look into. Start a file now. In years to come it will be invaluable.

SOURCES OF FISHING INFORMATION

The following list has been compiled for a ready source of up-to-date information on states, their laws and in many cases free booklets on where to go for each species of game fish. This information may be had for the asking.

Alabama—Department of Conservation, Administrative Building, Montgomery, Ala. 36101

Alaska—Department of Fish and Game, 229 Alaska Office Building, Juneau, Alaska 99801

Arizona—State Game and Fish Commission, Arizona State Building, Phoenix, Ariz. 85000

Arkansas—State Game and Fish Commission, Game and Fish Building, State Capitol Grounds, Little Rock, Ark. 72200

California—Department of Fish and Game, 722 Capitol Avenue, Sacramento, Calif. 95801

Colorado—State Game and Fish Department, 1530 Sherman St., Denver, Colo. 80200

Connecticut—State Board of Fisheries and Game, State Office Building, Hartford, Conn. 06100

Delaware—Board of Game and Fish Commissioners, Dover, Del. 19901

District of Columbia—Metropolitan Police, Washington, D.C. 20000

Florida—Game and Fresh Water Fish Commission, 646 W. Tennessee, Tallahassee, Fla. 32301

Georgia—State Game and Fish Commission, 401 State Capitol, Atlanta, Ga. 30300

Hawaii—Board of Commissioners of Agriculture and Forestry, Division of Fish and Game, Box 5425, Pawaa Substation, Honolulu, Hawaii 96800

Idaho—Department of Fish and Game, 518 Front St., Boise, Idaho 83700

Illinois—Department of Conservation, State Office Building, Springfield, Ill. 62700

Indiana—Department of Conservation Division of Fish and Game, 311 W. Washington St., Indianapolis, Ind. 46200

Iowa—State Conservation Commission, E. 7th & Court Ave., Des Moines, Iowa 50300

Kansas—Forestry, Fish and Game Commission, Box 591, Pratt, Kans. 67124

Kentucky—Department of Fish and Wildlife Resources, State Office Building, Annex. Frankfort, Ky. 40601

Louisiana—Wild Life and Fisheries Commission, 126 Civil Courts Building, New Orleans, La. 70100

Maine—Department of Inland Fisheries and Game, State House, Augusta, Maine 04330

Maryland—Maryland Game and Inland Fish Commission, State Office Building, Annapolis, Md. 21400

Massachusetts—Department of Natural Resources, Division of Fisheries and Game, 73 Tremont St., Boston, Mass. 02100

Michigan—Department of Conservation, Lansing, Mich. 48900

Minnesota—Department of Conservation, State Office Building, St. Paul, Minn. 55100

Mississippi—State Game and Fish Commission, Woolfolk State Office Building, Jackson, Miss. 39200

Missouri—State Conservation Commission, Farm Bureau Building, Jefferson City, Mo. 65101

Montana—State Fish and Game Commission, Helena, Mont. 59601

Nebraska—Game, Forestation and Parks Commission, State Capitol Building, Lincoln, Neb. 68500

Nevada—State Fish and Game Commission, Box 678, Reno, Nev. 89500

New Hampshire—State Fish and Game Department, 34 Bridge St., Concord, N.H. 03301

New Jersey—Department of Conservation and Economic Development, Division of Fish and Game, 230 W. State St., Trenton, N.J. 08600

New Mexico—State Department of Game and Fish, Santa Fe, N.M. 87501

New York—State Conservation Department, Albany, N.Y. 12200

North Carolina—Wildlife Resources Commission, Box 2919, Raleigh, N.C. 27600

North Dakota—State Game and Fish Department, Bismarck, N.D. 58501

Ohio—Department of Natural Resources, Wildlife Division, Ohio Department Building, Columbus, Ohio 43200

Oklahoma—Department of Wildlife Conservation, Room 118, State Capitol Building, Oklahoma City, Okla. 73100

Oregon—State Fish Commission, 307 State Office Building, Portland, Ore. 97200

Pennsylvania—State Fish Commission, Harrisburg, Pa. 17101

Rhode Island—Department of Agriculture and Conservation, Veterans Memorial Building, 83 Park St., Providence, R.I. 02900

South Carolina—State Wildlife Resources Department, 1015 Main St., Box 360, Columbia, S.C. 29200

South Dakota—State Department of Game, Fish and Parks, State Office Building, Pierre, S.D. 57501

Tennessee—State Game and Fish Commission, Cordell Hull Building, Nashville, Tenn. 37200

Texas—State Game and Fish Commission, Austin, Tex. 78700

Utah—State Department of Fish and Game, 1596 W. N. Temple, Salt Lake City, Utah 84100

Vermont—State Fish and Game Commission, Montpelier, Vt. 05602

Virginia—Commission of Game and Inland Fisheries, 7 N. 2nd St., Box 1642, Richmond, Va. 23200

Washington—Department of Game, 600 N. Capitol Way, Olympia, Wash. 98501

West Virginia—State Conservation Commission, State Office Building, No. 3, Charleston, W.Va. 25300

Wisconsin—State Conservation Department, State Office Building, Madison, Wis. 53700

Wyoming—State Game and Fish Commission, Box 378, Cheyenne, Wyo. 82001

MAPS THAT AID THE ANGLER

The U.S. government offers us the finest maps available. Each state is divided into small areas, and a separate map is available for each. Each stream, river and lake is shown in detail as are dirt roads and little-known access areas.

For maps east of the Mississippi River, contact the Geological Survey, Washington, D.C. West of the Mississippi, contact Geological Survey, Federal Center, Denver, Colorado.

Index maps of each state are available, free, which show all the quadrangles available for each area. From these master maps you may choose the individual area you wish to fish—then order it, by number, from Geological Survey for fifty cents per map.

CLEANING YOUR FISH

To Clean the Whole Fish (for Baking)

Remove dorsal fin and others by running knife along the spike bases where they join the backbone and cut away.

Cut away the tail and ventral and anal fins.

NAIL

By holding the head firmly (nail it to wood base if necessary) scale toward the head with a sharp knife.

OPENED FOR
GUTTING

Remove head, clean out guts and internal skin.

To Fillet the Fish

Start cutting along the back next to dorsal fin deep to the center line and around the bottom above fins.

Cut skin and flesh across base of tail and slide knife forward flat against the backbone all the way to the gill area.

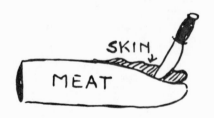

Remove all fins and inner skin. Pick up skin near the tail with knife and finger and rip forward.

GLOSSARY

ANTIREVERSE—Mechanism which allows line to be pulled from reel with handle remaining set.

AQUATIC INSECTS—Those born in the stream or lake and hatched to return to lay eggs, such as stone flies, mayflies, caddis flies.

BACKLASH—Line rolling over itself backward due to reel spool overspinning.

BAIT FISHING—Fishing with bait such as worms, minnows.

BAIT CASTING—A term used to describe the casting of plugs or lures which imitate bait fish.

BALANCED TACKLE—Tackle which balances well in hand and also that which, properly selected, performs to its ultimate.

BASS-BUG ROD—A staunch fly rod heavier than the usual trout weight to cast heavy bass flies and bug imitations long distances.

CREEL—Willow basket or canvas bag that holds the caught fish.

DRAG—On reel, controls the line flow from the reel spool.

FLIES, ARTIFICIAL—Those made to represent insects and bait fish on which the game fish feed.

GAME FISH—Designated fish species known for their game fighting qualities and also those under conservation law protection.

LEVEL-WIND MECHANISM—Winds the line on the reel spool evenly without the aid of the guiding fingers of your hand.

NONMULTIPLYING REEL—Single action, that is one revolution of the spool to one of the handle.

OFFSET HANDLE—Handle with the reel seat offset for better positioning for ease in fishing.

PANFISH—Small fish that fit in the frying pan.

PUSH-BUTTON REEL—Automatic line pickup and release mechanism on closed-face reels.

SINGLE-ACTION REEL—Nonmultiplying.

SNAP SWIVEL—A swivel with a snap attached to it for attaching leaders or additional terminal tackle or lures.

STRIKING—Pulling sharply on the line against the hit of a fish in order to set the hook in his mouth.

TAPERED LEADERS—Almost transparent leaders attached to the line and the end lure that taper from thick to thin in order to make the cast balance out in the air and float down on the water with minimum of disturbance (fly-fishing only).

TAPERED LINES—Lines tapered from thick to thin to balance the line in the air for best casting (fly-fishing only).

TERMINAL TACKLE—That which is attached to the end of the line: leaders, spreaders, sinkers, hooks, bobbers, lures.

THUMBING THE REEL—Controlling the outgo of the line by pressing on the spool during the cast (bait casting only).

TROLLING—Dragging the bait or lure behind a moving boat.

ULTRALIGHT TACKLE—The lightest and sportiest tackle practical for fishing conditions and fish species.

BIBLIOGRAPHY

Bates, Jr., Joseph. *Streamer Fly Fishing*. New York: D. Van Nostrand, 1950.

Bergman, Ray. *Trout*. New York: Alfred A. Knopf, 1959.

Brooks, Joe. *Complete Book of Fly Fishing*. New York: A. S. Barnes, 1958.

_____. *Complete Guide to Fishing Across America*. New York: Popular Science (Outdoor Life Book Club), 1966.

Crowe, John. *Modern ABC's of Freshwater Fishing*. Harrisburg, Pa.: Stackpole, 1973.

Evanoff, Vlad. *Freshwater Fisherman's Bible*. New York: Doubleday, 1964.

_____. *1001 Fishing Tips and Tricks*. New York: Harper and Row, 1966.

_____. *Another 1001 Fishing Tips and Tricks*. New York: Harper and Row, 1970 (paperback edition, New York: Hawthorn Books, 1975).

Flick, Art. *Art Flick's Master Fly Tying Guide*. New York: Crown, 1972.

Gabrielson, Ira. *New Fisherman's Encyclopedia*. Harrisburg, Pa.: Stackpole, 1963.

Lyons, Nick. *Fisherman's Bounty*. New York: Crown, 1970.

McClane, A. J. *American Angler*. New York: Holt, Rinehart & Winston, 1954.

Migdalski, Edward. *Anglers Guide to Fresh Water Fishes of North America*. New York: A. S. Barnes, 1962.

145

BIBLIOGRAPHY

Ovington, Ray. *Basic Fly Fishing and Fly Tying.* Harrisburg, Pa.: Stackpole, 1974.

_____. *How to Take Trout.* 1952. Reprint. New York: Freshet Press, 1975.

_____. *Introduction to Bait Fishing.* Harrisburg, Pa.: Stackpole, 1971.

_____. *Tactics on Bass.* New York: Alfred A. Knopf, forthcoming.

_____. *Tactics on Trout.* New York: Alfred A. Knopf, 1969.

INDEX

Accessories. 65-69
  fish keepers and bait boxes, 68-69
  footgear, 66
  jackets, 67
  lure containers, 67-68
  staff and nets, 68
  tackle box, 67-68
  water transportation, 65-66
Actions, fly-rod, 30
Alosa sapidissima (American shad), 114, 132-
  133
American Fishing Tackle Manufacturer's
  Association (AFTMA), 28
American shad (*Alosa sapidissima*), 114, 132-
  133
Anal fin, 116
Angle bait, 54
Antireverse mechanism, 143
Anus (of a fish), 116
Aquatic insects, 143
Artificial flies, 45-47, 143
  bass bugs. 46, 47
  categories of 45
Atlantic salmon (*Salmo salar*), 42, 125-126
Atlantic salmon fishing, 112-113

Backlash, 23, 143
Bait boxes, 68-69
Bait casting, 20-25, 143
  backlash, 23

difference between spin casting and, 23
drag-control button, 22
hand position, 21, 24
keeper ring, 23
level-wind mechanism, 21
putting tackle away, 18-19
reel, 22
retrieving the line, 24-25
rod grip, 20-23
straight and offset handles, 21, 23
striking, playing, and landing fish, 25
Bait fishing, 143
Baits, 45-54
  artificial, 45-52
  natural, 52-54
Balanced tackle, 143
Ball eye, 61
Bamboo fishing creel, 68-69
Bass-bug rod, 143
Bass bugs, 46, 47
Bass fishing, 86-97
  artificial lures for, 86-87
  largemouth, 87-92
  smallmouth, 92-97
  stream and river, 97
Bass species, 127-128
BB split shot, 56, 57
Bivisible trout fly, 46, 47
Black bass. *See* Largemouth bass
Blacknose dace as bait, 54
Bluegill, 70, 76, 134-135

Boat nets, 68
Braided metal leaders, 101
Brook trout (*Salvelinus fontinalis*), 117–119
Brown bullhead (*Ictalurus nebulosus*), 133–134
Brown trout (*Salmo trutta, S. Fario*], 119–120
Bubble or bobber, 59
Bucktail (or hair) fly, 46, 47
Bucktaillike wet-nymph fly, 46, 47
Buel, Julio, 86–87

Caddis fly as bait, 53
Care of tackle, 62–64
Casting, learning how, 5
Catfish, 76, 77, 133–134
Caudal fin, 116
Chain pickerel (*Esox niger*), 130–131
Channel catfish (*Ictalurus punctatus*), 134
Chars and Salmonoids. *See* Trout species
Cheek (of a fish), 116
Chest waders, 66
Chinook (*Oncorhynchus tshawytscha*), 124–125
Clamp-on type sinker, 56, 57
Cleaning your fish (for baking), 141
Clinch knot, 8
Closed-face reels for spinning, 8
    adjusting drag on, 11
    hand position, 11
Coho (*Oncorhynchus kisutch*), 125
Colorado spinner, 50, 72, 108, 114
Crappie, 70, 134–135
Crawfish as bait, 54
Creek chub as bait, 54
Creel, 68–69, 143
Curve cast, 37
Cutthroat and steelhead fishing, 109–110
Cutthroat trout (*Salmo clarki*), 121–122

Darter as bait, 54
Divided wing trout fly, 46, 47
Dolly Varden trout (*Salvelinus malma*), 122
Dorsal fin, 116
Double haul (or power cast), 39
Double taper fly-rod line, 28
Drag, 143
Dry trout fly types, 46, 47

Earthworms, 52, 54
Esox lucius (northern pike), 128–129

Esox masquinongy (muskellunge), 129–130
Esox niger (chain pickerel), 130–131
Eye (of a fish), 116
Eye hooks, 56, 57, 61

False cast fly-fishing, 35
Feathered hooks, 50
Feathered streamer fly, 46, 47
Fillet the fish, how to, 142
Fish catch, keeping, 68–69
Fish species, 115–135
    bass, 127–128
    catfish, 133–134
    diagram of (typical fish), 116
    number of, 115
    panfish, 134–135
    pike, 128–132
    salmon, 124–126
    shad, 132–135
    trouts, 116–124
    See also names of species
Fishing license, 69
Fishing tackle. *See* Tackle
Flatted needle eye, 61
Flatted shank, 61
Flexing action, spinning rod, 12
Flies, artificial, 45–47, 143
Floating fly lines, 28
Fly-fishing, 26–44
    actions, 30
    casts, learning to make, 31–36
        false cast, 35
        left (line) hand for control, 35
        steps in, 32–36
        wrist and arm motion (with line stripping),
            34
    fore-and-aft variations, 36–42
        curve cast, 37
        line retrieve in upstream fishing, 39
        power cast (or double haul), 39
        roll cast, 39–42
        roll-and-mend cast, 42
        roll-pickup cast, 38
        shooting the line, 37–38
    gear, setting up, 26–31
    leaders, 29
    lines, 28
    reels, 27
    striking, playing, and landing the fish, 42–44
    tackle, 27

Fly line, care of, 63
Footgear, 66
Fore-and-aft cast, variations on, 36–42
Frog as bait, 54

Game fish, 143
Gear
    for bait casting, 20–25
    care and repair of, 62–64
    for fly-fishing, 26–44
    setting up, 4–5
    for spin fishing, 7–19
Geological Survey maps, 140
Gill cover (of a fish), 116
Glossary of terms, 143–144
Grasshopper as bait, 54

Hackled fly, 46, 47
Hair-wing fly, 46, 47
Heddon, James, 87
Hellgrammite as bait, 96
Henshall, James, 86
Hip boots, 66
Hollow point hook, 61
Hook eyes, types of, 61
Hooks, 56, 57
    care of, 63
    types of, 61

Ictalurus nebulosus (brown bullhead), 133–134
Ictalurus punctatus (channel catfish), 134
Indiana spinner, 50, 74
Insect repellent, 69
Insects as bait, 53

Jackets, wading, 67
Johnson solid-mounted-hook spoon, 50

Keeper ring, 23
Killifish as bait, 54
Kirbed straight reversed hook, 61
Knobbed shank, 61
Knots, learning to tie, 58

Lake trout (Salvelinus namaycush), 123
Landlocked salmon (Salmo salar sebago), 126
Landlocked salmon fishing, 111

Largemouth bass (Micropterus salmoides), 128
Largemouth bass fishing, 87–92
    locations, 90
    lures and spoons, 91–92
    method for, 89–90
    principles of, 87–88
    rule of thumb for, 90
Lateral line (sense organs) of fish, 116
Lead strip wraparound lead, 56, 57
Leader loop, 56, 57
Leader size, recommended fly-rod action for, 30
Leaders, fly-fishing, 29
Level fly-rod line, 28
Level-wind mechanism, 143
    bait-casting reel, 21
Line, recommended spinning tackle for, 19
Line guides, on spinning rod, 12
Line stripping, fly-fishing, 34
Line taper, recommended fly-rod action for, 30
Live minnow, hooked (for still fishing), 56, 57
Looped eye, 61
Lower jaw (of a fish), 116
Lure containers, 67–68
Lure weights, recommended spinning tackle for, 19
Lures, 45–52
    bass bugs, 46, 47
    buying, 4
    categories of, 45
    plugs, 49–52
    pork chunk and rind, 45–52
    spinners and spoons, 48
    trout fly types, 46, 47
    worms and eels, 45–48

Mandible (of a fish), 116
Maps, 140
Marabou (trout fly), 46, 47
Marked shank, 61
Marked tapered shank, 61
Maxillary (of a fish), 116
Mayfly as bait, 53
Mayfly nymph (trout fly), 46, 47
Medicine kit, 69
Meek reel, 86
Metal leader, 56, 57
Micropterus dolomieu (smallmouth bass), 127
Micropterus salmoides (largemouth bass), 128
Muskellunge (Esox masquinongy), 129–130
    trolling for, 10–11, 25

Muskie and pike fishing, 100–102
    boat position, 101–102
    leaders for, 101
    recommended tackle for, 101

Natural bait, 52–54
    types of, 54
Needle eye, 61
Nets, 68
Nonmultiplying reel, 144
Northern pike (*Esox lucius*), 128–129
Nymphlike trout fly, 46, 47

Offset bend hook, 56, 57
Offset handle, 144
Offset handled rod for bait casting, 21
Oncorhynchus gorbuscha (pink salmon), 125
Oncorhynchus kisutch (coho), 125
Oncorhynchus nerka (sockeye), 125
Oncorhynchus tshawytscha (chinook), 124–125
Open-face reels for spinning, 8

Pacific salmon fishing, 113–114
    trolling, 10–11, 25
Pacific salmon species, 124–125
Palmer-tied fly, 46, 47
Panfish
    species, 70, 144
    meaning of, 134–135
Panfishing excursion (first trip out), 70–78
    at dock, 70–71
    procedure for, 71–78
    rowing out from the shore, 73–74
    spinning, 72–73
    trolling a spinning rod, 74–75
Pectoral fins, 116
Philippe, Samuel, 86
Pickerel fishing, 79–85
    bait, 80
    bait-casting reel, 83
    casting for, 80–81, 82, 85
    stripping out the line, 81–82
    trolling pattern, 82–83
Pike perch. *See* Walleyed pike fishing
Pike species, 128–132
    chain pickerel, 130–131
    muskellunge, 129–130
    northern pike, 128–129

trolling for, 10–11, 25
    walleye, 131–132
Pink salmon (*Oncorhynchus gorbuscha*), 125
Planning your trip, 13˝–142
    maps for, 140
    sources of information, 138–140
Plastic bubble or bobber, 59
Plastic worms and eels, 45–48
Playtl tapered leaders, 29
Plugs, 49–52
    types of, 51
Polaroid glasses, 67
Popping plugs, 51
Pork chunk and rind, 45–52
    types of, 49
Power cast (or double haul), 39
Push-button reel, 11, 144

Rainbow trout (*Salmo gairdnerii*), 120–121
Reels
    closed-face, 8, 11
    open-face, 8
    push-button, 11
    recommended fly-rod action for, 30
    recommended spinning tackle for, 19
    single-action, 144
Retrieving the line
    in bait casting, 24–25
    in spin fishing, 13–17
        casting sequence, 14
        correct positions for, 17
        line release, 16
        power cast, 15
Rigs, terminal tackle, 55–61
    hook chart, 61
    knots, 58
    plastic bubble or bobber, 59
    steelhead, 60
    uses and purposes, 57
Ringed hook, 61
River smallmouth fishing, 97
Rod flexing, for spinning, 12
Rod grip
    in bait casting, 20–21
    in fly-fishing, 31–32
    for spinning, 12–13
Rod length, recommended fly-rod action for, 30
Rods
    care of, 63
    recommended spinning tackle for, 19

Roll cast, 39–42
   in-stream position, 40
Roll-and-mend cast, 42
Roll-pickup cast, 38

Salmo clarki (cutthroat trout), 121–122
Salmo gairdnerii (rainbow trout), 120–121
Salmo gairdnerii (steelhead trout), 124
Salmo salar (Atlantic salmon), 42, 125–126
Salmo salar sebago (landlocked salmon), 126
Salmo trutta, s. fario (brown trout), 119–120
Salmon fishing, 111–114
   Atlantic salmon, 112–113
   casting, 112
   landlocked salmon, 111
   Pacific salmon, 113–114
   season for, 113
Salmon species, 124–126
   Atlantic, 125–126
   landlocked, 126
   Pacific, 124–125
Salvelinus fontinalis (brook trout), 117–119
Salvelinus malma (Dolly Varden trout), 122
Salvelinus namaycush (lake trout), 123
Sculpin as bait, 54
Shad, 132–133
Shad fishing, 114
Shank lengths, types of, 61
Shiner minnow as bait, 54
Silver salmon (*Oncorhynchus kisutch*), 125
Single-action reel, 14
Sinkers, care of, 63
Sinking fly lines, 28
Sinking plugs, types of, 51
Slip sinker, 56, 57
Small tools, 67–68
Smallmouth bass (*Micropterus dolomieu*), 127
Smallmouth bass fishing, 92–97
   bait, 96
   best location for, 96
   lure actions, 93–94
   retrieving and troll, 95
   stream and river, 97
   switching positions in boat, 94–95
Snap-swivel, 56, 57, 144
Snout (of a fish), 116
Snyder, George, 86
Sockeye (*Oncorhynchus nerka*), 125
Spear point, 61
Spider fly, 46, 47

Spin casting, difference between bait casting
   and, 23
Spin fishing, 1–19
   closed-face reels, 8
      adjusting drag on, 11
      hand position, 11
   dry run practice, 9
   line guides on rod, 12
   open-face reels, 8
   operating the tackle, 7–9
   perfecting casting, 9–17
   push-button reel, 11
   putting tackle away, 18–19
   recommended tackle for, 19
   retrieving the line, 13–17
      casting sequence, 14
      correct positions for, 17
      line release, 16
      power cast, 15
   rod flexing, 12
   rod grip, 12–13
   spool loading, 8
   striking, playing, and landing, 17–18
   synchro-drag, 11
   and trolling, 10–11
Spinners as lures, 48–49
   varieties of, 50
Split shots, 56, 57
Spool loading for spinning, 8
Spool types for spinning, 10
Spooners as lures, 48–49, 50
Squaretail. *See* Brook trout
Staff and nets, 68
Steelhead fishing, 109–110
Steelhead rigs, 60
Steelhead trout (*Salmo gairdnerii*), 124
Stickleback minnow as bait, 54
Stizostedion vitreum (walleyed pike), 131–132
Stone-fly (trout fly), 46, 47, 53
Stone-fly nymph bait, 53
Straight eye hook, 56, 57
Straight hook, 56, 57
Straight-handled rod for bait casting, 21
Stream insects and artificial imitations, 53
Stream smallmouth fishing, 97
Striking the line, 144
Strip lead trout fly, 46, 47
Sucker bait, 54
Sunfish, 70, 134–135
Surface-floating plugs, 51
Swivel combination and rig, 56, 57

Swivels, care of, 63
Synchro-drag, 11

Tackle
  buying, 3–4
  care and repair of, 62–64
  setting up the gear, 4–5
  terminal, 45–61
  See also Bait casting; Fly-fishing; Spin fishing
Tackle box, 4–5, 18, 67–68
Tandem-hooked streamer fly, 46, 47
Tapered eye, 61
Tapered leaders, 144
Tapered lines, 144
Tapered ring, 61
Tapered shank, 61
Terminal tackle, 45–61, 144
  basic rigs, 55–61
  lure selection and artificial flies, 45–52
  natural baits, 52–54
Thumbing the reel, 144
Tipped shank bent back, 61
Tipped spike bent back, 61
Trolling, 10–11, 144
  with spinning gear, 25
Trolling fin, 56, 57
Trout fishing, 102–108
  bait, 102–103, 107
  locations, 102
    and type of streams, 104–105
  objective in, 104
  rigs, methods, and direction of casting, 105–107
  spinning gear, 108
  in spring and fall, 104, 108
  in summer months, 108
Trout fly types, 46, 47
Trout species, 116–124

brook, 117–119
brown, 119–120
cutthroat, 121–122
Dolly Varden, 122
lake, 123
rainbow, 120–121
steelhead, 124
Turned down hooks, 61
Turned up hooks, 61

Ultralight tackle, 144

Ventral fins, 116

Waders, styles of, 66
Walleyed pike (*Stizostedion vitreum*), 131–132
Walleyed pike fishing, 97–100
  best areas to troll, 97–98
  jigs for, 99–100
  rod-tip motion and line retrieve, 100
  time of day for, 99
Water transportation accessories, 65–66
Weedless plug, 81
Weight, plumb-shaped, 56, 57
Weighted streamer-bucktail fly, 46, 47
Wet-style Palmer-like fly, 46, 47
White perch, 70, 75, 134–135
Winter steelheading, 109
Worms, plastic, 45–48
  types of, 48
Wulff heavy-hook trout fly, 46, 47

X-long shank two-lices hook, 61

Yellow perch, 70, 134–135
Yellow perch as bait, 54

Zigzagging plugs, 51, 87